Thomas
Cook

D1375306

ST
Bo
TEL: 0121-464 1534

Loans are up to 28 days. Fines are charged if items are not returned by the due date. Items can be renewed at the Library, via the internet or by telephone up to 3 times. Items in demand will not be renewed.
Please use a bookmark

Date for return

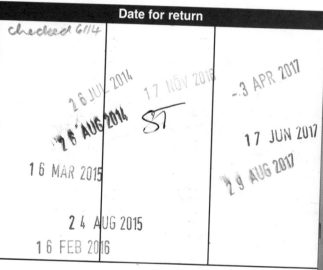

checked 6/14

2 6 JUL 2014   1 7 NOV 2016   -3 APR 2017

2 8 AUG 2014   ST   1 7 JUN 2017

1 6 MAR 2015   2 9 AUG 2017

2 4 AUG 2015

1 6 FEB 2016

Check out our online catalogue to see what's in stock, or to renew or reserve books.
www.birmingham.gov.uk/libcat
www.birmingham.bov.uk/libraries

Birmingham City Council

Q45612r1

Written by Teresa Fisher
Updated by Nadia Feddo

Published by Thomas Cook Publishing
A division of Thomas Cook Tour Operations Limited
Company registration No: 1450464 England
The Thomas Cook Business Park, 9 Coningsby Road
Peterborough PE3 8SB, United Kingdom
Email: sales@thomascook, Tel: +44 (0)1733 416477
www.thomascookpublishing.com

Produced by The Content Works Ltd
Aston Court, Kingsmead Business Park, Frederick Place
High Wycombe, Bucks HP11 1LA
www.thecontentworks.com

Series design based on an original concept by Studio 183 Limited

ISBN: 978-1-84157-884-2

First edition © 2006 Thomas Cook Publishing
This second edition © 2008 Thomas Cook Publishing
Text © Thomas Cook Publishing
Maps © Thomas Cook Publishing/PCGraphics (UK) Limited
Transport map © Communicarta Limited

Series Editor: Kelly Anne Pipes
Production/DTP: Steven Collins

Printed and bound in Spain by GraphyCems

Cover photography (Parc Güell) © Gräfenhain Günter/4Corners Images

CONTENTS

SYMBOLS KEY

The following symbols are used throughout this book:

ⓐ address ☎ telephone ⓕ fax ⓦ website address ⓔ email
🕐 opening times Ⓝ public transport connections ❶ important

The following symbols are used on the maps:

🛈	information office	▪	points of interest
🛫	airport	○	city
➕	hospital	○	large town
🛡	police station	○	small town
🚌	bus station	=	motorway
🚆	railway station	—	main road
Ⓜ	metro	—	minor road
✝	cathedral	—	railway
❶	numbers denote featured cafés & restaurants		

Hotels and restaurants are graded by approximate price as follows:
£ budget price **££** mid-range price **£££** expensive

Abbreviations used in addresses:
Av. Avinguda
C/ Carrer
Pl. Plaça

◉ *La Sagrada Família – a work in progress*

Introduction

Barcelona is one of the great Mediterranean cities. Dynamic, stylish and innovative, the capital of Catalonia boasts sun, sea, sandy beaches and some of the finest and most eccentric art and architecture in the world. Its unique urban landscape resembles a living museum. Even today, the city is a Mecca for the world's top architects, from local stars like Enric Miralles to international names such as Richard Rogers and Jean Nouvel, and their avant-garde structures sit comfortably alongside Gothic churches and dazzling *Modernista* edifices – the hallmark of the city.

It would be easy to spend a week simply paying homage to Barcelona's *Modernista* treasures, in particular those of its most famous son Antoni Gaudí. Throughout the world, people have marvelled at the creations and drawn inspiration from this great master. But the city abounds in sights and attractions that will appeal to all tastes, pockets and ages, including some of the finest galleries and museums in Europe. Barcelona is also home to La Rambla, one of the world's most famous boulevards. This is the street everyone visits, talks about and tries to photograph or paint. It is more theatre than thoroughfare but it is nonetheless a vital part of the city's makeup – this is where Barcelona's heart beats loudest.

A massive facelift prior to the 1992 Olympics converted the previously provincial, old city into a chic, cosmopolitan metropolis bursting with pride and self-confidence. The transformation of the derelict seafront rejuvenated the city, reminding the Barcelonans of their maritime heyday, and giving rise to the slogan Barcelona *oberta al mar* (Barcelona open to the sea). More recent coastline projects include events such as the 2004 Forum of Cultures, which provided a vast new entertainment and leisure area at the north-eastern end of the city; and the Hotel Vela, a sail-shaped luxury hotel and leisure complex intended to sex up the rather dilapidated old fishing docks of the Barceloneta. Now Barcelona is considered the 'style capital of Europe', exuberant and sophisticated, with world-class shopping, an exceptional cultural scene and a flamboyant nightlife. Remember, this is the European capital that never sleeps – tonight doesn't usually start until tomorrow.

Today, Barcelona continues to reinvent itself district by district, celebrating its past by restoring its old buildings, while at the same time remaining at the forefront of contemporary culture. It is the richest, fastest-growing, most creative and most stylish city in Spain – and what's more, its motto is *Barcelona Es Teva* (Barcelona belongs to you).

🔺 *A view of the city from La Sagrada Família*

When to go

SEASONS & CLIMATE

Barcelona has no low season as there are always things going on. The best time to visit, however, is late spring/early summer, when the weather is warm but not too hot, and the street life is at its most vibrant.

The coldest season is winter, with an average temperature of 10°C (54°F). Snow is rare and days are generally mild but damp, with the occasional day of clear blue skies and bright crisp sunshine.

In spring the average temperature is around 15°C (59°F). These are some of the wettest months but, from late March onwards, the weather starts to warm up. After Easter, outdoor café tables become more popular and by May it is usually warm enough to eat alfresco in the evenings.

During summer, the average temperature is around 25°C (75°F), but it can reach 37°C (99°F) in July and August when the humidity can make the city feel oppressively hot and muggy. Although there is little rain, the occasional sudden violent thunderstorm provides a brief but refreshing respite from the heat.

Early autumn is an ideal time to visit, with generally mild sunny weather. The average autumn temperatures are around 16°C (53°F). By mid-October, the fine weather becomes more intermittent, with frequent heavy rainfalls, and the pavement tables disappear until spring.

ANNUAL EVENTS

Throughout the year, religious processions, festivals and traditions turn the city of Barcelona into an open-air theatre. Here are some of the highlights.

● *Gaudí's rippling* trencadís *benches in Parc Güell*

January

New Year Barcelonans eat 12 grapes for luck to the chimes of midnight. The *Reis Mags* (Wise Men) arrive by boat to tour the city on 5 January, showering the crowd with sweets. Children traditionally receive their Christmas presents now, or lumps of sugar coal if they've misbehaved.

February

Feast of Eulàlia On 12 February, the feast day of St Eulàlia is celebrated with a week of traditional parades, *gegants* (giant figures), concerts, *sardanes* (Catalan folk dance) and *castellers* (human castles).

Carnestoltes A week of colourful pre-Lenten parades ends on Ash Wednesday with the symbolic burial of a sardine on Barceloneta beach.

March–April

Setmana Santa Easter sees church services and processions throughout the city, particularly by the Gothic Catedral on Palm Sunday; godparents buy godchildren a *mona*, or cartoon chocolate sculpture.

Sant Jordí (St George; 23 Apr) This local alternative to St Valentine's Day is when sweethearts exchange gifts – a rose for the woman and a book for the man. La Rambla becomes a huge outdoor bookshop.

Corpus Christi Parades of giants and dancing *capgrossos* (big heads), and the 18th-century tradition of *Ou com Balla* (dancing egg): an empty eggshell balances on the Catedral's fountain to symbolise the Eucharist.

June–July

Sónar A three-day music and multimedia festival. Ⓦ www.sonar.es

Sant Joan festivities Summer solstice bonfires, the *Nit del Foc* (night of fire) in Barceloneta and all-night beach parties.

De Cajón A new flamenco music festival. Ⓦ www.deflamenco.com

B-estival Soul, R&B and blues festival. Ⓦ www.b-estival.com

August–September
Festa Major Gràcia's streets compete for the best decorations and entertainment; carrer Verdi is always impressive. The finale sees fireworks and a *correfoc* (fire run) – devils and dragons scattering firecrackers.
La Mercè (17–24 Sept) The grandest fiesta, devoted to the Virgin of Mercy. Four days of celebrations climax with the Ball de Gegants, where 5m-high giants dance from Drassanes to Ciutadella, followed by a *correfoc*.

November–December
Festival Internacional de Jazz One of Europe's most prestigious jazz festivals. Ⓦ www.the-project.net
Christmas festivities The Santa Llúcia craft fair is outside the Catedral (2–23 December) and a large nativity scene is set in Plaça Sant Jaume.

PUBLIC HOLIDAYS

New Year's Day 1 January	**Catalan National Day** 11 September
Epiphany 6 January	*La Mercè* 24 September
Good Friday 21 March 2008, 10 April 2009	**Discovery of Americas** 12 October
Easter Monday 24 March 2008, 13 April 2009	**All Saints' Day** 1 November
May Day 1 May	**Constitution Day** 6 December
Whit Monday 12 May 2008, 1 June 2009	**Immaculate Conception** 8 December
St John's Day 24 June	**Christmas Day** 25 December
Assumption Day 15 August	**St Stephen's Day** 26 December

Gaudí & *Modernisme*

The *Modernisme* movement – a taste for what is modern –
emerged in Barcelona at the turn of the 19th century with the
aim of breaking away from the past through new art forms.
It was Spain's home-grown interpretation of art nouveau and,
thanks to its greatest exponent, Antoni Gaudí, Catalan *Modernisme*
had the greatest impact, influencing all forms of European art,
architecture, literature and theatre and making Barcelona
a veritable open-air museum of *Modernista* style.

● *The dragon's back and saint's cross at Casa Batlló*

No single architect has ever marked a major city quite as comprehensively and spectacularly as Gaudí did in Barcelona. For many people, Gaudí alone is sufficient reason to visit Barcelona. He designed many of its most charismatic buildings; throughout the city mansions, parks, schools, gateways, lampposts and sculptures provide a constant reminder of his genius. His innovative work represents a flamboyant fusion of structure and decoration, giving precedence to use of colour and light within architectural forms. His remarkably organic structures are frequently adorned with his trademark pinnacles, towers and rooftop terraces. Particularly striking are **Casa Milà** (see page 90), with its extraordinary rippling façade devoid of straight lines and right-angled corners, and **Casa Batlló** (see page 93), an imaginative example of the fusion of architecture with the decorative arts of the époque. The green, blue and ochre mosaics of this enigmatic building symbolise the scaly skin of the dragon, its knobbly roof the dragon's back, the balconies represent the skulls and bones of its victims, while the tower shows St George's cross.

However, Gaudí's most emblematic structure is the still unfinished **Temple Expiatori de la Sagrada Família** (see page 96), the city's iconic temple that he spent over 40 years creating, personally going out into the street to raise funds among the passers-by to facilitate its construction. 'The patron of this project is not in a hurry' he once remarked. Tragically, in 1926 he was run over by a tram on the Gran Via and died unrecognised in hospital. When his identity was eventually discovered, Barcelona gave him what was almost a state funeral. His body is fittingly buried in the crypt of the Temple, to which he devoted his life.

GAUDÍ'S BARCELONA HIGHLIGHTS

Casa Batlló (see page 93)
Parc Güell (see page 94)
Palau Güell (see page 107)
La Sagrada Família (see page 96)
Casa Milà 'La Pedrera' (see page 90)

History

ORIGINS OF THE CITY

According to legend, Hercules founded Barcelona in 2000 BC on his colonial expedition from Africa aboard nine boats: *barça* (boat), *nona* (nine). In fact, it was the Carthaginians who first established a stronghold here around 230 BC, allegedly naming the city *Barcino* after Hannibal's father, Hamil Barca. The Carthaginians were swiftly followed by the Romans in about 15 BC. However, the rise of Barcelona's fortunes coincided with the decline of the Roman Empire and the invasion of the Visigoths in 531. In 878, Guifré el Pilós (Wilfred 'The Hairy') founded the independent country of Catalonia. He named himself the first Count of Barcelona, thereby founding a dynastic line that was to rule an increasingly powerful nation for several centuries.

THE MEDIEVAL CITY

During the early Middle Ages, Barcelona flourished during its brief Moorish occupation, until the Christians took Barcelona in 1229 under Catalan King Jaume I. The city became a powerful naval base and trading centre – one of the three most important merchant cities in the Mediterranean, along with Genoa and Venice. The lavish medieval mansions of the old town – former residences of the Counts of Barcelona and the Kings of Catalonia and Aragón – together with such impressive new buildings as the Catedral, the church of Santa Maria del Mar and the Drassanes shipyards, stand as testimony to this golden age. In the 15th century, Catalonia became a self-governing region, and built its own parliament buildings in Barcelona. However, from the 16th to the 18th centuries, as Spain's economic focus turned away from the Mediterranean to the colonisation of the Americas, Barcelona experienced a period of economic decline and, during the Spanish War of Succession, Catalonia lost its autonomous status.

THE CATALAN RENAIXENÇA

During the 18th century, Catalonia began to re-emerge, thanks to a steady growth in agriculture, textiles, wine production and shipping. The 19th-century industrial revolution created new prosperity in Barcelona, making it the fastest expanding city in Spain. This also brought about a cultural 'renaissance', as Catalan language and literature began to flourish once more.

Hand in hand with the cultural renaissance came the *Modernisme* movement (the Catalan offshoot of art nouveau). Ildefons Cerdà designed the grid-like Eixample district to house the burgeoning middle classes, while *Modernista* architects like Gaudí designed the district's apartment buildings and mansions.

BARCELONA TODAY

The 20th century brought Barcelona new challenges, including the Franco dictatorship from the end of the Spanish Civil War until 1975, during which time Catalan national identity was repressed. However, the 1992 Olympic Games provided a boost for the city and the transformation of the down-at-heel waterfront was one of the most popular aspects of the city's radical revamp, an effort that has continued with ambitious projects such as the 2004 Forum of Cultures.

Today, the city goes from strength to strength, renovating and reinventing itself district by district, with La Ribera, El Born, El Raval and most recently, La Barceloneta, emerging as newly fashionable quarters. Barcelona keeps its reputation as a forward-looking city at the forefront of design and contemporary culture.

Lifestyle

Barcelonans are fiercely proud of their unique Catalan culture and will repeatedly inform you that Catalonia and its capital city are not Spanish. Indeed they will even try to convince you that Barcelona, not Madrid, is Spain's premier city and, in their eyes, it really is.

Their pride in their city and in their regional culture is manifested in every aspect of daily life – in their cuisine (see page 24) and in

● *Casa Beethoven, a music shop on La Rambla*

their language. Although Barcelona still has two official languages, Catalan and Castilian Spanish, *Català* has completely taken over on public signage and is spoken as the everyday language by over a third of the city's population and understood by over 90%. Even the city's celebrated football team, FC Barça, represents so much more than just a football club. During the Franco era, it was a rallying point for Catalans at matches against their arch rivals, Real Madrid, and it became the focus of their hatred of central government. At the height of the dictatorship, match results were pre-ordained so that Madrid would win. Still today, whenever they play Real Madrid, all of Spain is gripped, and should Barça win, the streets of Barcelona erupt to the sound of car horns, fireworks and popping cava corks.

Barcelonans certainly know how to enjoy themselves, and no month goes by without a festival, a fiesta or a public holiday. But they are also hard-working and prosperous. In a recent survey, Barcelona's economic progress was ranked third among cities of the world. Punctuality is important for meetings, and formal wear is the norm. Business hours are generally 08.00 or 09.00 until 18.00 or 19.00, with a lengthy lunch break between 13.30 and 15.30 or 16.00 to include an afternoon siesta during hotter months. These days, more and more companies are switching to a more European 9-5 timetable to facilitate international business.

Barcelonans rarely invite guests into their home. As in many Mediterranean countries, they prefer to socialise in the city's 2,500 bars, cafés and restaurants. Eating is regarded as one of life's great pleasures, and mealtimes are often lengthy gatherings with all the family. And there is no denying that Barcelonans are night owls. The city's intoxicating club scene is among the best (and the latest) in Europe. Here evening begins when most people elsewhere have already gone to bed – clubs rarely open before 3am.

Culture

Barcelona is one of Europe's great cities, thanks mainly to its rich cultural heritage and the dynamism of the contemporary arts and design scene. It is exceptional for the quantity and quality of museums and galleries in proportion to its size – with over 50 to choose from, together with a busy calendar of music and arts events in theatres and concert venues throughout the city, not to mention an impressive range of street artists and entertainers.

Make the informative Museu d'Història de la Ciutat (City History Museum), the lively Museu d'Història de Catalunya (History Museum of Catalonia) or the fascinating Museu Marítim (Maritime Museum) your first port of call. Once you have a grasp of the city's colourful history, walks around town are all the more rewarding. If you intend to visit several museums, it is worth getting a *Barcelona Card* (valid for two to five days), which offers discounts of 10–100 per cent at the city's main museums, together with free travel on public transport.

The city galleries showcase some dazzling permanent collections by three of the prime movers and shakers in Spanish modern art – Pablo Picasso, Joan Miró and Antoni Tàpies. The Museu Nacional d'Art de Catalunya spans several centuries with its remarkable displays, which include one of the world's most important collections of Romanesque art and an impressive selection of Modernist *objets d'art*, while the Museu d'Art Contemporani de Barcelona contains some striking contemporary art. Art aficionados should buy an *Articket*, a multi-ticket providing half-price admission to seven of the city's foremost art centres: MNAC, Fundació Joan Miró, Fundació Antoni Tàpies, CCCB, MACBA, La Pedrera and Museu Picasso. Tourist offices

● *Sculpture at the Fundació Joan Miró*

provide the Ruta del Modernisme guide, covering 115 *Modernista* buildings in Barcelona and Catalonia marked by the small red circles on the pavement outside. Valid for a year, it contains discounts of 15–50 per cent. The Ruta del Disseny guide covers the city's 100 best-designed buildings with nine separate itineraries.

Barcelona also boasts some of the world's finest and most eccentric architecture. Its extraordinary urban landscape resembles a living museum, from the ancient Gothic quarter, built within the Roman city walls – a honey-coloured maze of dark, narrow alleys and charming, hidden squares – to the regimental grid plan of the turn-of-the-century Eixample district, studded with its many eye-catching jewels of *Modernista* architecture, and beyond to the space-age constructions of more recent years.

A showcase for the best of Spain's theatrical talent, the city is home to such renowned troupes as *Els Comediants*, *La Fura dels Baus*, *Els Joglars* and *El Tricicle*. It is also famed for its wide diversity of musical events from classical music, opera and ballet through jazz, pop and rock, to some of the most innovative music festivals in Europe. In 1999 the city opened the Auditori arts centre (home to the National Catalan Orchestra) and regained its prestigious opera house, the Gran Teatre del Liceu, whose season runs from October until mid-July, with ballet staged during summer months. Another major classical music venue, the Palau de la Música Catalana – a *Modernista* gem – is worth visiting whatever the programme.

One of the most important annual musical events is the 'Grec' Summer Festival, staged at the Teatre Grec on Montjuïc hill – an ambitious open-air programme of theatre, music and dance. Other festivals are devoted to jazz, flamenco and contemporary music.

◗ *Rooftop chimneys at Casa Milà 'La Pedrera'*

Shopping

As a leading European city of fashion and design, Barcelona offers a wealth of shopping opportunities, from designer boutiques to quirky speciality shops, small district markets to glitzy department stores. It offers a unique shopping experience, cleverly fusing tradition and innovation, and its main interior design stores and small, eccentric boutiques make the hunt for gifts here especially enjoyable.

Best buys include clothing, shoes and decorative goods. Look for local designers Antoni Miró, Josep Font and Lydia Delgado for fashions; and designers, André Ricard, Ricardo Bofill and Javier Mariscal.

Start your spending spree in the Eixample district, where the grid-like streets are lined with chic interior design shops and prestigious

⬟ *The Maremàgnum complex in Port Vell*

fashion emporia. The most exclusive are brilliant for window-shopping: Passeig de Gràcia and La Rambla de Catalunya; the Avinguda Diagonal between Plaça Joan Carles I and Plaça Francesc Macià.

Old-fashioned arts and crafts shops juxtapose more off-beat boutiques in the intimate streets and alleyways of the Barri Gòtic. Try Carrer Banys Nous for arts and antiques; Carrer Petritxol for art galleries, home accessories and gift ideas; and Carrer Portal de l'Angel and Carrer Portaferrissa for high-street fashion chains and shoes.

The newly trendy neighbouring districts of La Ribera and El Born contain myriad tiny craft workshops, jewellers and designer boutiques, as well as some superb art galleries in the streets around Museu Picasso. El Corte Inglés is the city's only real department store, with several different locations (notably Plaça Catalunya, Carrer Portal de l'Angel, and Plaça Francesc Macià), and the waterfront also attracts shoppers to the Maremàgnum shopping centre and the new Diagonal Mar mall. In late 2007 the shopping spotlight will be on the futuristic new shopping and leisure complex designed by Richard Rogers from the old Les Arenes bullring in Plaça d'Espanya.

Larger shops tend to open 09.00 to 21.00 Monday–Saturday. Smaller shops close during the siesta (13.00–16.30), early on Saturdays and frequently on Mondays. Some shopping centres (including the Maremàgnum) open on Sundays, and food shops and markets generally open early in the morning. There are 40 covered municipal markets across the districts of the city but the most famous, La Boqueria, is centrally placed on La Rambla and is one of the best places to stock up on picnic supplies or even have a quick tapa or two. Two recently rebuilt markets are in the Barceloneta, which reopened in March 2007 with a solar roof, and the Mercat de Santa Caterina in the Born, famous for its wavy, mosaic-studded roof designed by Enric Miralles. Both have high-quality restaurants.

Eating & drinking

Don't let Barcelona's dazzling cultural scene divert you from its culinary excellence. The city boasts a huge culture of eating, drinking and conversation, with lengthy lunches and late night dining, and a bewildering choice of eateries from spacious designer brasseries to tiny neighbourhood tapas bars.

⬤ *Dishing up paella in La Barceloneta*

WHEN TO EAT

Barcelonans enjoy good food and often eat out. It is customary in Catalonia to eat late, with lunch served typically from 14.00 to 16.00, aperitifs and tapas in the early evening, then dinner from 21.30 to midnight or later. Many cafés and bars remain open from early morning until late at night. It is advisable to book in most restaurants, especially at weekends. Most offer a fixed price *menú del día* (fixed lunch menu), which is usually good value but restrictive. The *à la carte* menus generally offer some of the more unusual dishes and regional specialities. Prices on the menu include 7 per cent VAT (*IVA*), unless stated, and it is customary to tip by rounding up the bill after a meal, or to add on 5–10 per cent if you are feeling generous.

WHAT TO EAT

There is no such thing as Spanish 'national cuisine' but it is possible to taste various local styles, including Galician and Basque. The majority of restaurants serve the regional cuisine, *la cuina Catalana* – a Mediterranean style of cooking, with bold, sun-drenched flavours in hefty portions.

Traditional Catalan dishes lean heavily on olive oil, tomatoes, garlic, peppers, aubergines, courgettes and herbs which, when mixed, form *samfaina*, a delicious sauce served with meat and fish dishes. Other sauces include romesco (nuts, tomatoes and spicy red pepper) and *allioli* (a strong mayonnaise-type blend of garlic and

PRICE CATEGORIES

The price guides indicate the approximate cost of a three-course meal for one, excluding drinks, at the time of writing.
£ up to €25 ££ between €25 and €50 £££ above €50

olive oil). Pork is the mainstay of the Catalan diet, although chicken, rabbit, duck, beef and game are popular too. Meats are often cooked with fruit in such delicacies as *pollastre amb pera* (chicken with pears) and *conill amb prunes* (rabbit with prunes). Seafood is hugely popular, from simply grilled sardines to a hearty *sarsuela* (seafood stew). Try the local variant on *paella*, called *fideuà* (using pasta noodles rather than rice) and the eye-catching shellfish platters. Catalan cuisine is unique within Spain for mixing fish and meat

USEFUL DINING PHRASES

I would like a table for ... people
Quisiera una mesa para ... personas
Keyseeyera oona mesa para ... personas

May I have the bill, please?
¿Podría traerme la cuenta
por favor?
*¿Pordreea trayerme la cwenta
por farbor?*

Waiter/waitress!
¡Camarero/Camarera!
¡Camareroe/Camarera!

Could I have it well-cooked/medium/rare please?
¿Por favor, la carne bien hecha/al punto/poca hecha?
¿Por fabor, la kahrrne beeyen echa/al poontoh/poka echa?

I am a vegetarian. Does this contain meat?
Soy vegetariano. ¿Lleva carne este plato?
Soy begetahreeahnoh. ¿Yevah carneh esteh plahtoh?

together to create such exotic dishes as *sepia amb mandonguilles* (squid with meatballs) and *mar i cel* (sea and heaven) – a combination of sausages, rabbit, prawns and fish.

The best-known Catalan dessert is *crèma catalana* (cream custard topped with caramelised sugar). Look out also for *mel i mató* (fresh cheese with honey); *postre de músic*, simply a handful of mixed nuts and dried fruit with a glass of amaretto; and *coques* (pastries sprinkled with sugar and anything from pine nuts to candied fruit or pork fat).

Don't miss the excellent locally produced wine and sparkling *cava* from the Penedès, Priorat or the Costers del Segre regions.

WHERE TO EAT

The Barri Gòtic and Gràcia contain a variety of small, atmospheric restaurants that are generally reasonably priced. Eateries on La Rambla tend to be overpriced and touristic. The Eixample is slightly more upmarket, and contains some excellent tapas bars, and there are plenty of intimate candlelit bistros and fashionable brasseries to be found in La Ribera, El Born and, increasingly, in El Raval. For seafood, head to the Olympic Port or to the atmospheric fishing district of La Barceloneta.

TAPAS

Tapas bars abound throughout the city, serving savoury snacks with a pre-meal drink to *tapar el apetito* (to put a lid on the appetite). If you are overwhelmed by the mouth-watering counter displays, simply point to one or two tempting dishes or order a *tapa combinada* – a bit of everything!

Entertainment & nightlife

Barcelona is a city of night owls, and the vibrant club scene is among the best in Europe. There is plenty to choose from every night, and weekends here begin on Thursday. A typical evening begins around 20.30 with tapas and aperitifs in a local bar, followed by a leisurely dinner around 22.30. The usual starting time for opera, ballet and concerts is around 21.00, or 22.00 for theatre. After midnight, music bars become crowded. Around 03.00 the clubs and discos fill up and the famous Barcelonan night movement sweeps across the city until dawn. For those who just don't want to stop, there are 'afters' bars that take the party all the way to lunchtime the next day.

The main nightlife areas are El Born and La Ribera, with their many small bars, and the chic nightspots of L'Eixample. However, the Barri Gòtic and El Raval are also lively and some of the more exclusive bars and clubs are further afield – on Montjuïc hill and the lower slopes of Tibidabo.

The city's flamboyant club scene caters to all tastes, although house and electronic beats take centre stage at present. Many of the clubs are on the European circuit for celebrated DJs and live bands, and there is even an annual Sónar festival of experimental electronic music and technology in June, attracting all the big names in digital sound. During summer the beachfront clubs often have outdoor dancing, and some inland clubs have fantastic dance terraces, some with swimming pools. There are also numerous Latin clubs featuring salsa, merengue and samba beats. Entry to the top clubs is not cheap, so look out for free entry passes at various bars around the city centre or discount flyers, which are sometimes handed out on La Rambla at night. The city also boasts numerous live music venues, ranging from vast rock and pop arenas to traditional flamenco clubs and mellow, intimate jazz bars featuring artists from all over the world.

There's a wide-ranging programme of classical music, ballet and dance, staged in such impressive venues as the beautiful *Modernista* Palau de la Música Catalana and the Gran Teatre del Liceu. Throughout the year, recitals are staged in churches, museums and monasteries, and during summer months in some of the city parks, including Ciutadella Park, Parc Güell and the Teatre Grec on Montjuïc hill,

● *A tempting display at one of Barcelona's many tapas bars*

which stages an open-air summer festival of theatre, music and dance. Barcelona's theatre programme is unlikely to appeal to visitors, unless you speak Catalan or Spanish, in which case there is the full spectrum from classical to avant-garde on offer. Several cinemas show screenings in the original version with subtitles.

Tickets are best purchased from the relevant box office at each venue. Alternatively, you can book by phone or via the internet and collect the tickets at the venue, from Servi-Caixa (❶ 902 332 211 Ⓦ www.serviticket.com) and Tel-Entrada (❶ 902 101 212 Ⓦ www.telentrada.com) – operated by two of the city's largest

BARS & CLUBS

The best source of local entertainment listings is the magazine *Guía del Ocio* (Ⓦ www.guiadelociobcn.es). It previews cinema, theatre, music and nightlife for the week, together with extensive sections on bars, restaurants and the city's thriving gay scene. The most comprehensive English-language guides are *Barcelona Metropolitan Magazine* (Ⓦ www.barcelona-metropolitan.com) and *Barcelona Connect* (Ⓦ www.barcelonaconnect.com), both free in pubs, bars, tourist offices and language centres. For on-line listings in English try *Lecool magazine* (Ⓦ www.lecool.com) and the city council's excellent website (Ⓦ www.bcn.es). The local paper, *La Vanguardia* (Ⓦ www.lavanguardia.es) also has an arts and entertainments page. The leaflet *Informatiu Musical*, available free from tourist offices, record shops and concert venues, is an excellent source of concert and recital information. There is also a cultural information desk at Palau de la Virreina (Ⓔ La Rambla 99 ❶ 933 017 775).

savings banks, La Caixa and Caixa Catalunya. Servi-Caixa has special machines next to La Caixa's ATMs, which print out the tickets; Tel-entrada is operated out of larger branches of Caixa Catalunya, and at a dedicated desk in the Plaça de Catalunya tourist office.

🔺 *Street sculpture* – Barcelona Head *by Roy Lichtenstein*

Sport & relaxation

SPECTATOR SPORTS

Barcelonans are football crazy and no visit to the city is complete
for sports fans without a visit to Camp Nou, home to FC Barcelona
(W www.fcbarcelona.com) and one of the great shrines of world
football. Other celebrated city teams include the 'Barcelona Dragons'
(W www.fcbarcelonaweb.com/dragons), who play in the World
League of American Football on Sundays from April to June at the
Estadi Olímpic; DKV Joventut (W www.penya.com) and FC Winterthur
Barcelona (W www.fcbarcelona.com) are the top basketball teams,
which play league games on Sunday evenings and European and
Spanish Cup matches midweek from September to early June at
the Pabellón Olímpico (Olympic Pavilion) in Badalona and the Palau
Blaugrana respectively; and FC Barcelona Pista de Gel, the city's ice

● *Windsurfing on Barceloneta beach*

HOW TO GET TICKETS

Tickets for major sporting events are available from venues, at ⓦ www.serviticket.com or www.barcelona-ticket-office.com.

hockey team, which plays at the ice rink of the Camp Nou complex (ⓐ Av. Joan XXII ⓣ 934 963 630 ⓦ www.fcbarcelona.com).

Bullfighting is not popular in Barcelona although the city still has two bullrings: Les Arenes in the Plaça d'Espanya and El Monumental on Carrer Marina. Les Arenes was left derelict for many years but has reopened as a leisure centre. Monumental is still in business but the fights, catering to tourists and the local population of Andalucían immigrants, are of a notoriously low standard.

PARTICIPATION SPORTS

The Centre Municipal de Tennis Vall d'Hebron (ⓐ Passeig de la Vall d'Hebron 178 ⓣ 934 276 500) has clay courts open to the public, while Squash Barcelona (ⓐ Av. del Doctor Maranón 17 ⓣ 933 340 258) is the city's largest squash complex, with 14 squash courts and two racket-ball courts. Book ahead.

Several clubs offer weekend sailing and windsurfing courses. Contact Base Nàutica de la Mar Bella (ⓐ Av. Litoral ⓣ 932 210 432 ⓦ www.basenautica.org). The Olympic Piscina Bernat Picornell (ⓐ Avenida de l'Estadi 30–40 ⓣ 934 234 041) and the seafront Club de Natació Atlètic Barceloneta (ⓐ Pl. del Mar ⓣ 932 210 010) are two of several swimming pools open to the public.

Contact the sports information service (ⓐ Avenida de l'Estadi 30–40 ⓣ 934 023 000) for details of city-run sports centres and facilities.

Accommodation

Barcelona offers a wide range of hotels, from cool, contemporary boutique and deluxe belle époque palace, to simple B&Bs and hostels. Luxury hotels are generally extremely expensive; quality budget accommodation can be difficult to find even during winter months.

Many affordable hotels are located in the atmospheric Barri Gòtic. Those on or near La Rambla may be noisy at night. The Eixample offers a wider selection, especially in the mid-range price bracket, but these often sacrifice character for functionality. There are no campsites in the city but there are plenty of centrally located youth hostels for budget travellers. Apartment hotels are a good bet for extended stays, especially if you're travelling as a family.

Early booking is essential and breakfasts are usually charged on top. All hotel bills are subject to 7 per cent VAT. There is usually a charge for secure hotel car parking. It is virtually impossible to find a hotel off the street so, if you haven't booked in advance, try the hotel-finding agency Ultramar Express (☏ 934 914 463 🕔 08.00–22.00) in Sants railway station, or the main tourist office (☏ 933 043 232 🕔 09.00–21.00) in Plaça de Catalunya.

HOTELS

Banys Orientals £ The ultimate in urban chic, surprisingly affordable for the heart of fashionable El Born. ⓐ C/ Argenteria 37 ☏ 932 866 460 ⓦ www.hotelbanysorientals.com Ⓜ Metro: Jaume I

Jardí £ A popular small hotel on one of the Barri Gòtic's most atmospheric squares. Book well in advance for a room with a view. ⓐ Pl. Sant Josep Oriol 1 ☏ 933 015 900 Ⓜ Metro: Liceu

PRICE CATEGORIES
The ratings below (unrelated to the official star system) indicate the approximate cost of a room for two people for one night (excluding VAT and breakfast):
£ up to €100 ££ €100–199 £££ over €200

Market Hotel £ Right by the Sant Antoni market, this sleek monochrome hotel is high on design but low on price and comes with a great restaurant. ❸ C/Comte Borell 68 ❶ 933 251 205 ⓦ www.markethotel.com.es ⓝ Metro: Sant Antoni

Casa Camper ££ A concept boutique hotel from the Camper footwear company with starkly modern décor and plenty of treats such as organic breakfasts, hammocks and bikes for rent. ❸ C/ Elisabets 11 ❶ 933 422 680 ⓦ www.casacamper.com ⓝ Metro: Catalunya

Colón ££ Cosy old-fashioned hotel opposite the cathedral – an excellent choice for families. ❸ Avenida de la Catedral 7 ❶ 938 450 636 ⓦ www.hotelcolon.es ⓝ Metro: Jaume I or Urquinaona

Condes de Barcelona ££ Elegant hotel combining *Modernista* architecture with avant-garde décor. ❸ Passeig de Gràcia ❶ 934 450 000 ⓦ www.condesdebarcelona.com ⓝ Metro: Diagonal

Hotel 54 Barceloneta ££ Spanking new hotel by the beach with unbeatable views of the city, a roof lounge terrace and hip décor in shades of understated grey. ❸ Passeig Joan de Borbo 54 ❶ 932 252 054 ⓦ www.hotel54barceloneta.com ⓝ Metro: Barceloneta

Neri ££ An intimate boutique hotel with state-of-the-art amenities within a characterful 18th-century palace in the Barri Gòtic. ⓐ C/ Sant Sever 5 ⓣ 933 040 655 ⓦ www.hotelneri.com ⓜ Metro: Jaume I or Liceu

Arts £££ Fashionable hotel beside the sea in one of Spain's tallest buildings, with high-tech facilities and spa. ⓐ C/ de la Marina 19–21 ⓣ 932 211 000 ⓦ www.harts.es ⓜ Metro: Ciutadella or Vila Olímpica

La Florida £££ The ultimate romantic getaway – a 5-star historic hotel with post-modern interiors on Tibidabo, with sensational spa, pool and gardens overlooking the city. ⓐ Carretera Vallvidrera al Tibidabo 83–93 ⓣ 932 593 000 ⓦ www.hotellaflorida.com

H1898 £££ Very smart 4-star hotel in a majestic 19th-century building bang on the Rambla, with a spa, pools and gym. ⓐ La Rambla 109 ⓣ 935 529 552 ⓦ www.nnhotels.es ⓜ Metro: Catalunya

Omm £££ Cutting-edge boutique hotel with minimalist interiors, relaxation centre, nightclub, rooftop pool and celebrated restaurant. ⓐ C/ Rossello 265 ⓣ 934 454 000 ⓦ www.hotelomm.es ⓜ Metro: Diagonal

GUESTHOUSES

Hostal Gat Raval £ A funky budget *hostal* in the heart of the Raval, with sparkling clean communal bathrooms, views of the MACBA and bright, sunny rooms. ⓐ C/ Joaquín Costa 44, 2nd floor ⓣ 934 816 670 ⓦ www.gataccommodation.com ⓜ Metro: Universitat

Sagrada Família £ A tiny B&B for those seeking home comforts. ⓐ C/ Nápols 266 ⓣ 933 174 342 ⓦ www.sagradafamilia-bedandbreakfast.com ⓜ Metro: Sagrada Família

YOUTH HOSTELS

Centric Point £ Modern youth hostel with broadband, bar, satellite TV and breakfast included. ❸ Passeig de Gràcia 33 ❶ 932 312 045 ⓦ www.centricpointhostel.com ⓝ Metro: Passeig de Gràcia

◔ *The striking Hotel Arts enjoys a wonderful beachside location*

THE BEST OF BARCELONA

There's plenty in Barcelona to fill even a long city break but if you have only a few days to spare then here's our list of sights and experiences you should really try not to miss.

TOP 10 ATTRACTIONS

- **La Sagrada Família** This eccentric temple is an architectural marvel, the symbol of the city and Gaudí's most celebrated creation (see page 96)

- **Museu Picasso** A comprehensive collection of early artworks by Pablo Picasso, from childhood sketches to Cubism, housed in five medieval palaces (see page 80)

- **Museu Nacional d'Art de Catalunya (MNAC)** One thousand years of Catalan art under one roof – don't miss the decorative arts and photography displays (see page 114)

- **Manzana de la Discordia** Just one block holds three *Modernista* masterpieces: Gaudí's *Casa Batlló*, Puig i Cadafalch's *Casa Ametller* and Domènech i Montaner's *Casa Lleó Morera* (see page 92)

- **Parc Güell** Antoni Gaudí's flamboyant hilltop park is an extraordinary piece of landscape design, great for family picnics and far-reaching views (see page 94)

- **Fundació Joan Miró** A dazzling gallery devoted to one of Barcelona's finest artists up on Montjuïc hill (see page 111)

- **La Rambla** The most famous boulevard in Spain and the hub of city life for locals and visitors alike (see pages 58 & 62–4)

- **El Born and Santa Maria del Mar** The city's 'seaside church' is striking in its simplicity. You'll find it in the trendy El Born area of the city (see pages 75 & 79)

- **Palau de la Música Catalana** One of the city's greatest *Modernista* masterpieces, an internationally acclaimed concert hall and a UNESCO World Heritage Site (see page 81)

- **Camp Nou** Home of FC Barcelona. If you can't get a ticket for a match, at least visit the museum and take a tour of the stadium (see page 122)

◐ *Detail of the old ticket offices at the Palau de la Música*

Suggested itineraries

Here's a quick guide to seeing the best of Barcelona, depending on the time you have available.

HALF-DAY: BARCELONA IN A HURRY

If you have only a few hours, start your visit promenading with locals along the city's most famous boulevard, La Rambla. Then explore the dark atmospheric streets and enchanting squares of the Barri Gòtic. Art lovers should also visit the remarkable collections of Museu Picasso in the neighbouring La Ribera district.

1 DAY: TIME TO SEE A LITTLE MORE

Having completed the half-day itinerary, you are now at the heart of the fashionable La Ribera district with its myriad hip fashion

● *La Rambla, Spain's most famous boulevard*

boutiques, galleries and design shops, so add some shopping to your day. Alternatively, visit the beautiful church of Santa Maria del Mar or take in a museum. The Museu d'Història de Catalunya is especially interesting. For dinner, head back to the trendy bars and bistros of La Ribera or enjoy more traditional dishes and some of the city's finest seafood in the Barceloneta district.

2–3 DAYS: TIME TO SEE MUCH MORE

These extra days provide plenty of time to explore the city's museums and spectacular *Modernista* architecture. The Eixample district contains many of the most famous buildings. Shopaholics will also enjoy Passeig de Gràcia – the Champs Elysées of Barcelona – for its exclusive shops and designer boutiques. There are also some excellent tapas bars here for a light lunch, before heading off to admire Gaudí's most celebrated sights – La Sagrada Família and Parc Güell.

Or visit Montjuïc hill and spend the day marvelling at such major museums as the Museu Nacional d'Art de Catalunya (MNAC) and the Fundació Joan Miró. Return to the old town for dinner in the Barri Gòtic. You may also have time to explore the rejuvenated waterfront, including Port Vell with its impressive Maremàgnum shopping complex and the ancient royal shipyards of the Museu Marítim.

LONGER: ENJOYING BARCELONA TO THE FULL

A longer stay enables you to soak up the café culture of the old town, to top up your tan on the beaches and to visit some of the outlying districts of town, including Pedralbes with its monastery and museums, and Mont Tibidabo in the Collserola hills. For out of town trips, see page 130.

Something for nothing

Barcelona is an excellent city for budget travellers, with plenty of free sights and attractions. For a taste of Barcelona's history, stroll the narrow maze of alleyways of the medieval Barri Gòtic district; explore the 'open-air museum' district of L'Eixample to marvel at the *Modernista* architecture of the early 20th century; and visit Montjuïc hill to admire the high-tech sporting facilities of the 1992 Olympics. Some museums offer free entry once a month (including Museu Picasso, Museu Frederic Marès and Museu d'Història de Catalunya on the first Sunday of the month, and MNAC on the first Thursday of the month). In many ways, the entire city resembles a giant outdoor gallery, with over 400 open-air monuments and sculptures to enjoy.

Shopping fanatics on a budget can enjoy some of the world's finest window-shopping, especially on Passeig de Gràcia, the Diagonal and in La Ribera and El Born. There are also several worthwhile markets to browse, including an antiques market in Plaça del Pi on Thursdays; the weekend art market in Plaça Sant Josep Oriol; the Sunday coin and stamp market in Plaça Reial; the huge flea market of Els Encants at Glòries; and the sensational food market of La Boqueria from Monday to Saturday.

Alternatively, escape the bustle of downtown Barcelona and walk in the Collserola hills or head for the city's beautiful parks. Relax in tranquil Parc de la Ciutadella or admire the sweeping city vistas and unusual sculptures of Gaudí's Parc Güell. Many parks contain playgrounds and attractions for children, including Parc de l'Espanya Industrial with its giant dragon slide and a small boating-lake, and Parc del Laberint with a fun topiary maze. The city squares are also great places to sit and watch the world go by: feed the pigeons in Plaça de Catalunya; listen to the buskers in Plaça de Sant Josep Oriol;

and watch the *sardana* dancers perform in Plaça de la Seu on Saturday at noon and 18.00 or Plaça Sant Jaume on Sunday at noon too. It's also fun to people-watch on La Rambla, and enjoy the lively street entertainment every few paces, ranging from buskers and card sharps to human statues. And on lazy summer days, where better to while away the hours than on Barcelona's fine, sandy beaches?

🔺 *Take a siesta in Parc Güell*

When it rains

It rarely rains in Barcelona. On average the city has 300 days of sunshine each year and the tendency is for brief showers rather than day-long downpours. It is more likely that you will want to spend time indoors to get out of the heat than the rain. However,

PLAZA DE TOROS MONUMENTAL

Domingo Tarde, 5.30

ACONTECIMIENTO TAURINO
con la presentación de las Señoritas Toreras

● *Escape the elements in the Museu Tauri, the bullfighting museum* come rain or shine, there are plenty of indoor activities to keep you amused.

There are over 50 museums and galleries catering for all ages and interests, from highbrow modern art to football. Immerse yourself in history at the Museu d'Història de la Ciutat or the Museu Marítim; visit one of numerous art galleries, including Museu Picasso, Fundació Joan Miró, the Museu Nacional d'Art de Catalunya and the Museu d'Art Contemporani de Barcelona; or seek refuge from the elements in the Catedral, the Basílica de Santa Maria del Mar or the Monestir de Pedralbes. Children especially enjoy the underwater world at L'Aquàrium; the state-of-the-art IMAX cinema at Port Vell; and Cosmocaixa, the new hands-on science museum and planetarium on the lower slopes of Tibidabo.

Barcelona's shopping ranks among the best in the world, and there are several large department stores and shopping centres to occupy any keen shopper for hours, including El Corte Inglés, Spain's main department store, with branches throughout the city; Maremàgnum at Port Vell; and a number of exclusive shopping malls off Passeig de Gràcia and Rambla de Catalunya.

If that sounds too energetic, relax at a beauty spa. The Six Senses Spa at Hotel Arts and the ZenZone Spa at the Gran Hotel La Florida offer the ultimate in pampering. Or join locals in one of the numerous bars and cafés. Take your pick of refreshment in spacious trendy 'design-bars'; *xampanyerías* (champagne bars); cosy old-fashioned bodegas, serving wine from the barrel; traditional tapas bars; and *cervecerías* (beer bars). Or simply master the Barcelonan art of coffee drinking in one of the characterful locals' cafés: try *cafè amb llet* (a large milky coffee) for breakfast; a *tallat* (a small coffee with a dash of milk) or a *cafè* (espresso) at midday; and a *cigaló* (an espresso with a shot of brandy unless you specify another liqueur) after dinner.

On arrival

ARRIVING
By air

Barcelona's airport, El Prat de Llobregat (☎ 932 983 838 Ⓦ www.aena.es) is situated 12 km (8 miles) southwest of Barcelona. The best way to reach the city centre from the airport is by taxi. This takes around 20–30 minutes but it is the most expensive option. There is also a regular Aerobús bus service every 8-15 minutes (06.00–01.00 Mon–Fri, 06.30–01.00 weekends) from the airport to Plaça de Catalunya, via Plaça d'Espanya, Gran Via de les Corts Catalanes and Plaça de la Universitat. Tickets are available from the driver and the journey takes about 30-40 minutes. The return ticket is valid for a week.

At rush hour, the regular rail service (06.00–23.44 daily) is a quicker option. Cross the walkway form Terminals A and B to the station where the C1 train leaves at 29 minutes and 59 minutes past the hour. It runs to Estació Sants, Urquinaona, Arc de Triomf and Clot-Aragó, all of which connect with the metro.

By rail

The city's main railway station, Estació Sants (ⓔ Pl. dels Països Catalans ① 934 956 215), is the main arrival point from both national and international destinations, which also connects with the metro network. Facilities include tourist information, hotel information, a bank, restaurants, shops, first-aid and left-luggage lockers. Other

🔻 *Awaiting arrivals at Barcelona's airport*

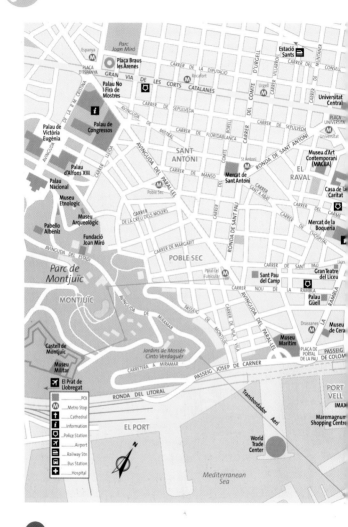

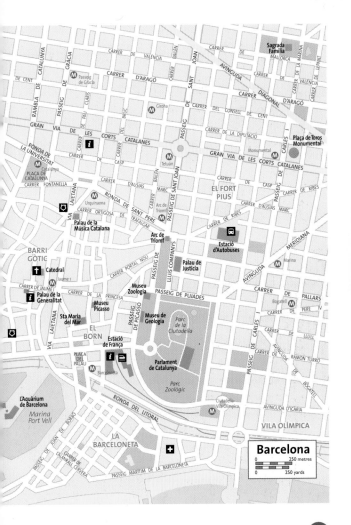

major railway stations in the city include Estació de França
(🅐 Avenida Marqués de l'Argentera), near Barceloneta metro
station, and Estació Passeig de Gràcia, near Plaça de Catalunya.

By road

Eurolines (🅣 902 405 040 🅦 www.eurolines.es) provide coach links
with most major Spanish cities, and arrive into Estació del Nord
(🅐 Av. Vilanova 🅣 902 260 606). Coaches from foreign cities generally
arrive into Estació Autobuses de Sants (🅐 C/ Viriato 🅣 934 904 000),
beside the main Sants railway station.

If you are driving, the A7 motorway is the main route to Barcelona
from France, while the A2 joins Zaragoza to the west, with connections
from Madrid. The Barcelona ring road makes it easy to approach the
city centre from all directions but, once in the centre, driving can be

---

IF YOU GET LOST, TRY SOME CASTILLIAN SPANISH

Excuse me, do you speak English?
Perdone, ¿habla usted inglés?
Perdoene, ¿ahbla oosteth eengless?

**Excuse me, is this the right way to the old town/the city centre/
the tourist office/the station/the bus station?**
Perdone, ¿por aquí se va al casco antiguo/al centro de la ciudad/
a la oficina de turísmo/la estación de trenes/estación de autobuses?
*Perdoneh, ¿porr akee seh bah ah el kasko antigwo/al thentroe
de la theeoodath/a la offeetheena deh toorismoe/la estatheeon
de trenes/estatheeon dey awtoebooses?*

quite daunting with fast multi-lane avenues and complicated one-way systems. Parking can also be difficult and car parks are expensive. Your best bet is to find a space marked in blue with a *Zona Blava* (Blue Zone) sign and to purchase a ticket from a nearby parking meter. Parking costs around €2–4 per hour.

FINDING YOUR FEET

Barcelona appears to be a bustling Mediterranean city but the pace of life here is surprisingly relaxed. As with most major cities, there are incidents of petty crime, so it is advisable to take common sense precautions (see page 145).

ORIENTATION

Barcelona is easy to navigate as it's divided into districts, each with distinctive characteristics, and the public transport system is efficient. You may get lost in the labyrinth of narrow streets and dark alleys of the Barri Gòtic and La Ribera, but that is half the fun. Arm yourself with a good map and make sure you know where the boundary thoroughfare of Via Laietana is located! L'Eixample can be a little confusing as it's built on a grid system with extremely long avenues and identical-looking blocks of buildings. There are certain unmissable landmarks, though, such as the sea, Montjuïc hill and Mont Tibidabo.

GETTING AROUND

The metro network, operated by TMB (Ⓦ www.tmb.net), is the most efficient means of transport in the city. It is easy to use, with seven lines, each identified by a number and a colour, and the direction is indicated by the end-station of each line. The metro runs 05.00–24.00 Mon–Thur and Sun, 05.00–02.00 Fri, 24 hours on Saturdays and public holidays.

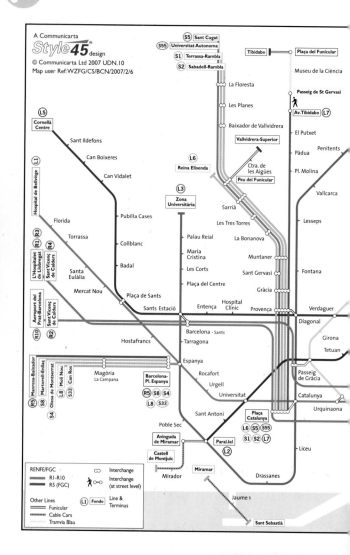

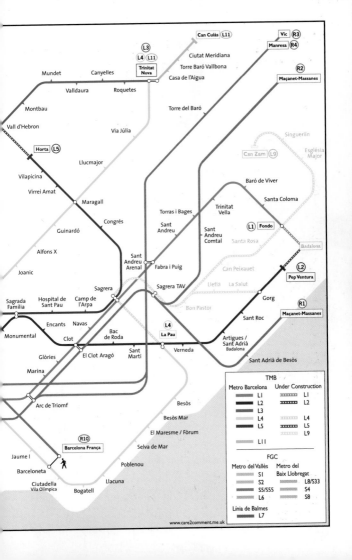

www.care2comment.me.uk

For the suburbs and surrounding areas there are regional rail lines run by the Ferrocarrils de la Generalitat de Catalunya – FGC (Ⓦ www.fgc.es) and RENFE. The FGC line is fully integrated into the metro system and runs 05.45–24.00 Mon–Thur, 05.50–02.15 Fri–Sat and 05.50–24.00 Sun, although times can vary for different lines. The main station for regional trains is Plaça de Catalunya (underground, at the top of La Rambla). Buy tickets from ticket offices and automatic vending machines at each station. Remember to validate your ticket in a machine on the platform before boarding.

There is also an extensive bus network, operated by TMB (06.30–22.00), with most services passing through Plaça de Catalunya, Plaça Urquinaona or Plaça de la Universitat. Purchase your tickets from the driver and validate in the machines on the buses. The city's 16 night-bus routes, which run approximately every half-hour from 23.00–04.00, require separate tickets.

If you intend to use the bus and metro frequently, consider one of the special multi-ride tickets available from metro ticket offices, automatic vending machines and FGC railway stations. These include the T-10 for 10 journeys; a T-día one-day pass and also special tourist passes, valid for two, three, four and five days, which cover all transport in the city, including the journey to and from the airport. The Barcelona Card offers unlimited use of public transport for up to five days and discounts on the Aerobús and cable cars along with reduced entry to various museums and attractions.

The Bus Turístic is an easy way to get around, with 42 hop-on-hop-off stops. There are two main routes, North and South, which embrace all the main city sights, starting from Plaça de Catalunya and lasting about 2 hours. The buses run every 6–20 minutes, depending on the season, from 09.00–19.00 (until 20.00 Apr–Oct), except 25 Dec and 1 Jan, passing every 5–25 minutes depending on the season.

A third route introduced in 2007 covers the Fòrum area and runs Apr–Sept, 09.30–19.00. Tickets are available for one or two days and cost €19 for an adult, €11 for children aged 4-12.

Look out also for the TombBús – a special shopping service that runs every 7 minutes on weekdays (07.30–21.58) and every 15 minutes on Saturdays (09.30–21.45) between Plaça de Catalunya and Plaça Pius XII.

Other modes of public transport include the funicular railway up Montjuïc from Avinguda Paral.lel to Avinguda Miramar from 09.00–20.00 (22.00 in summer), with a Telefèric (cable car) leading up to Montjuïc

● *Street art on Montjuïc hill*

castle from 11.00–19.15; another cable car, the Transbordador Aeri, runs from Barceloneta to Miramar, a peaceful lookout point over the city, 10.30–19.00 (Mar to mid-June), 10.30–20.00 (mid-June to mid-Sept), 10.30–19.00 (mid-Sept to mid-Oct) and 10.30–17.30 (mid-Oct to Feb); the Golondrinas pleasure boat tours (see page 77); the ancient *Tramvia Blau* (Blue Tram) from FGC Avinguda Tibidabo to Plaça Doctor Andreu (see page 124); and the Funicular de Tibidabo (see page 124).

Black-and-yellow taxis can be hailed in the street or booked in advance, but they are an expensive option. Those that are free have a green light on the roof and a sign saying *lliure/libre* in the front window. Reliable companies include Radio Taxi (❶ 933 033 033) and Servitaxi (❶ 933 300 300). Alternatively, hire a bicycle from Un Coxte Menys (❷ C/ Esparteria 3 ❶ 932 682 105) at around €5 an hour or €15 a day.

A new eco-friendly way to get around the city is the Trixi rickshaws (Ⓦ www.trixi.com ❶ 93 310 1379), which run 12.00–20.00 Apr–Sept and can be booked by phone or hailed on the street, usually from around the Catedral or near the beach.

CAR HIRE

It's only worthwhile hiring a car if you're planning to explore Catalonia. There are several car rental companies at the airport, although pre-booking with your airline's affiliates should secure you reduced rates.

Avis ❷ Terminals B & C ❶ 932 983 601 Ⓦ www.avis.es
Europcar ❷ Terminals B & C ❶ 932 983 300 Ⓦ www.europcar.es
Hertz ❷ Terminals B & C ❶ 932 983 637 Ⓦ www.hertz.es
National Atesa ❷ Terminals B & C ❶ 932 983 433 Ⓦ www.atesa.es

▶ *La Barceloneta waterfront*

La Rambla & Barri Gòtic

Sooner or later, all visitors to Barcelona find themselves strolling
with locals on La Rambla, Spain's most famous and well-trodden
boulevard, abuzz with market stalls, artists and street entertainers.
It leads through the heart of the old city down to the port. Just off
La Rambla, the Barri Gòtic (Gothic Quarter) is Barcelona's oldest
district, brimming with atmospheric streets, alleyways and hidden
squares, and flanked by countless buildings of historical interest.
The Barri Gòtic is something of a misnomer as the district combines
its splendid Gothic architecture with Roman, Romanesque and
Renaissance elements, making it a fascinating area to explore.

SIGHTS & ATTRACTIONS

Monument a Colom

This monumental column at the seaward end of Las Ramblas is
crowned by a statue of Christopher Columbus, pointing to the
horizon with an outstretched arm. It commemorates the great
navigator's return to Barcelona from his first voyage to the Americas
in 1492. It was erected outside the naval headquarters of Catalonia
during the 1888 Universal Exhibition and from the top it affords
spectacular views of the seafront. ❸ Pl. del Portal de la Pau
❶ 933 025 224 ❺ 09.00–20.30 Ⓝ Metro: Drassanes

Plaça de la Seu (Cathedral Square)

More commonly known as Plaça Nova (new square) or simply Plaça
de la Catedral, this spacious square is a popular meeting point and
also draws a number of buskers and street entertainers. On Sundays,
locals gather at 12.00 and 18.00 to perform the *sardana*, a curiously

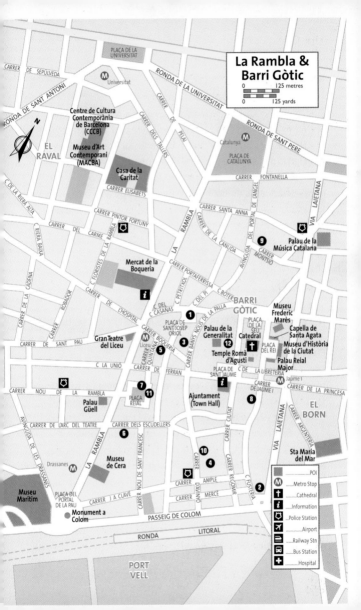

La Rambla & Barri Gòtic

| 0 | 125 metres |
| 0 | 125 yards |

PLAÇA DE LA UNIVERSITAT

CARRER DE SEPÚLVEDA

RONDA DE LA UNIVERSITAT

RONDA DE SANT ANTONI

Universitat

CARRER DE PELAI

CARRER DES TALLERS

RONDA DE SANT PERE

Catalunya

PLAÇA DE CATALUNYA

EL RAVAL

Centre de Cultura Contemporània de Barcelona (CCB)

Museu d'Art Contemporani (MACBA)

Casa de la Caritat

CARRER ELISABETS

CARRER FONTANELLA

CARRER PINTOR FORTUNY

CARRER SANTA ANNA

LA RAMBLA

CARRER DE LA CANUDA

AVINGUDA DEL PORTAL DE L'ANGEL

Palau de la Música Catalana

VIA LAIETANA

C DE LA RIERA ALTA

CARRER DEL CARME

CARRER DE LA CANUDA

CARRER MONTSIÓ

C DE LA RIERA BAIXA

Mercat de la Boqueria

CARRER PORTAFERRISSA

BARRI GÒTIC

Museu Frederic Marès

Capella de Santa Àgata

CARRER DE L'HOSPITAL

PLAÇA DE SANT JOSEP ORIOL

Palau de la Generalitat

PLAÇA DE LA SEU

Catedral

Museu d'Història de la Ciutat

Gran Teatre del Liceu

Liceu

Temple Romà d'Agustí

PLAÇA DEL REI

Palau Reial Major

CARRER DE FERRAN

PLAÇA DE SANT JAUME

CARRER DE LA LIBRETERIA

Jaume I

CARRER DE LA PRINCESA

C LA UNIÓ

CARRER NOU DE LA RAMBLA

Palau Güell

PLAÇA REIAL

Ajuntament (Town Hall)

CARRER DE JAUME I

EL BORN

CARRER DELS ESCUDELLERS

Museu de Cera

CARRER NOU DE SANT FRANCESC

Sta Maria del Mar

CARRER DE L'ARC DEL TEATRE

CARRER DAVINYÓ

CARRER RECOMÀ

VIA LAIETANA

Drassanes

AVINGUDA DE LES DRASSANES

PLAÇA DEL PORTAL DE LA PAU

Museu Marítim

CARRER J A CLAVÉ

CARRER AMPLE

CARRER MERCÈ

Monument a Colom

PASSEIG DE COLOM

RONDA

LITORAL

PORT VELL

	POI
M	Metro Stop
✝	Cathedral
i	Information
☒	Police Station
✈	Airport
▤	Railway Stn
▤	Bus Station
✚	Hospital

> **WHAT'S IN A NAME?**
> The name 'Rambla' is derived from *ramla* (Arabic for 'sand'),
> named after the sandy stream bed here that ran parallel with
> the medieval city walls, carrying rainwater down to the sea.
> Dry during summer months, this route soon became the
> main link to the harbour. In the 14th century, it was eventually
> paved. Such is its significance today that the Barcelonans have
> coined two new words – *ramblejar*, to walk down the Rambla
> and *ramblista*, someone who loves to *ramblejar*.

sedate Catalan folk dance, before the Cathedral's ornate and
imposing façade (under renovation until 2008). Between the east
side of the Cathedral and Via Laietana lie the remnants of the
ancient Roman walls. **ⓐ** Pl. de la Seu **Ⓜ** Metro: Liceu or Jaume I

Plaça de Sant Jaume

This square is situated on the site of the former forum and marketplace
of Roman *Barcino*. Today it represents the city's political hub. On its
south side stands the impressive Catalan Gothic **Ajuntament**
(Town Hall), seat of the city's government.

The first floor contains the famous old council chamber, the Saló
de Cent (Chamber of One Hundred), with its patriotic tapestries.
Across the square, the Renaissance **Palau de la Generalitat**
(Government Palace) is home to the government of Catalonia.
ⓐ Pl. de Sant Jaume **Ⓜ** Metro: Jaume I

▶ *Human statue outside the Catedral*

Plaça del Rei

The delightful 'King's Square' was once a busy medieval marketplace. Today it is a fascinating ensemble of architectural styles. One side is occupied by the **Palau Reial Major** (Great Royal Palace), the former residence of the Counts of Barcelona, constructed in the 11th century. It was on the steps leading up to the palace that King Ferdinand and Queen Isabella are believed to have received Columbus on his return from the Americas in 1493. On the north side of the square, the Gothic **Capella de Santa Àgata** (Chapel of St Agatha) was constructed on the old Roman wall. Opposite, the **Palau del Lloctinent** (Palace of the Viceroy) was built in 1549 for the Catalan representative of the king. There are marvellous views of the medieval city from the top of the five-storey **Mirador de Rei Martí** (Tower of King Marti). The **Museu d'Història de la Ciutat** (City History Museum, see page 65) is also in the square. ❸ Pl. del Rei Ⓜ Metro: Jaume I

Plaça Reial

This charming porticoed square, flanked by bars and restaurants and adorned by palm trees and an ornamental fountain, was constructed in 1848. Some of the façades are decorated with sculpted terracotta reliefs of celebrated navigators and the two tree-like central lampposts were Gaudí's first commission in Barcelona. On Sunday mornings there is a coin and stamp market here. Be warned that at night it can get a little scuzzy and there is a high presence of pickpockets. ❸ Pl. Reial Ⓜ Metro: Liceu

La Rambla

This magnificent 18th-century tree-lined promenade – with its cafés, buskers, newsstands, street artists and bustling crowds of locals and tourists – is where the city's heart beats loudest. La Rambla is among the Mediterranean's most celebrated boulevards, and the pride of Barcelona, although even its most ardent fans admit that it has become a little down-at-heel of late. Part of the council's recent clean-up campaign has included the renovation of the Miró floor mosaic outside the Liceu opera house, a greater police presence to deter the pickpockets and quality controls on the human statues and artists. La Rambla is also known as Les Rambles/ Las Ramblas as it is divided into five sections, each with its own characteristics. Descending from Plaça de Catalunya they are: Rambla de Canaletes, named after the famous little iron fountain – one sip allegedly ensures your return to the city; Rambla dels Estudis, colloquially known as Rambla dels Ocells because of the bird stalls; Rambla de Sant Josep, also called Rambla de les Flors because of the flower stalls and best known for the Boqueria market and Liceu opera house; Rambla dels Caputxins;

⬤ *Charming Plaça Reial, constructed in 1848*

and Rambla Santa Mònica, which is filled with caricature artists.
a La Rambla Metro: Catalunya, Liceu or Drassanes

Temple Romà d'Agustí

Housed in headquarters of the Catalan hiking club lies one of the great secrets of Roman Barcelona, virtually unvisited by the hordes of nearby tourists: four jaw-dropping fluted Corinthian columns dating from the first century BC. Historians agree that they once formed the back corner of the Temple to Augustus and stood at the very heart of the Forum of Roman *Barcino*. Marking the central spot is an old millstone just by the entrance of the building. **a** C/ Paradís 10
i 933 151 111 **⏱** 11.00–18.00 Mon–Fri, 11.00–15.00 Sat & Sun
Metro: Jaume I

CULTURE

Catedral

Barcelona's mighty Gothic Cathedral was constructed on the remains of a palaeo-Christian basilica and a Romanesque church. Dedicated to St Eulàlia, who was martyred by the Romans in the 4th century for her Christian beliefs, it is considered one of the finest examples of Catalan Gothic architecture.

The majestic interior is a harmonious fusion of medieval and Renaissance style, and the Chapel of Christ of Lepanto is its finest example of Gothic architecture. Eulàlia herself lies in the subterranean alabaster crypt below the altar. Don't miss the tranquil 14th-century cloister, with its shaded gardens, pond and even a small gaggle of 13 white Roman geese, representing Eulàlia's age and the 13 grisly punishments meted out to her by the Roman emperor. **a** Pl. de la Seu
i 933 151 554 **⏱** 08.00–13.15, 16.30–19.30 Metro: Liceu or Jaume I

Gran Teatre del Liceu

For over 150 years, the Liceu has been Spain's foremost opera house, hosting world-class performers from Montserrat Caballé to José Carreras ever since its inauguration in 1847. However, it has an extremely chequered history: it was tragically burned down in 1861, and rebuilt only to be bombed in 1893. It was restored to its former glory, then went up in flames again in 1994. Once more it rose from the ashes in 1999, but this time with improved acoustics, a larger stage and state-of-the-art machinery. Guided tours of the interior provide a unique insight into the workings of the theatre. ⓐ La Rambla 51–59 ⓘ 934 859 914 ⓦ www.liceubarcelona.com ⓛ Guided tours at 10.00 (1 hour); 'express' tours at 11.30, 12.00 & 13.00 (20 minutes) ⓜ Metro: Liceu

Museu d'Història de la Ciutat (City History Museum)

This fascinating museum recounts the city's evolution through 2,000 years of history, in a series of locations around the **Plaça del Rei** (see page 62). Start at the impressive underground walkways beneath the square, which reveal the ancient foundations of the Roman settlement of *Barcino*.

The main section of the museum is housed in a medieval mansion, and vividly traces the story of Barcelona from a simple Roman trading post to a wealthy 18th-century metropolis. The museum ticket also includes entry to the **Saló del Tinell**, the spacious barrel-vaulted banqueting hall of the **Palau Reial Major**; the royal chapel, the **Capella de Santa Àgata**; and the **Mirador del Rei Martí**. ⓐ Pl. del Rei, C/ del Veguer 2 ⓘ 933 151 111 ⓦ www.museuhistoria.bcn.es ⓛ 10.00–20.00 Tues–Sat, 10.00–15.00 Sun, June–Sept; 10.00–14.00, 16.00–20.00 Tues–Sat, 10.00–15.00 Sun, Oct–May. Also night visits: 21.00–23.30 Mon–Tues, July; 21.00–23.30 Tues–Wed, Aug–Sept ⓜ Metro: Jaume I

Museu Frederic Marès (Frederic Marès Museum)

This eccentric museum, at the heart of the Gothic Quarter, was founded and donated to the city by sculptor and private collector of all manner of curios, Frederic Marès i Deulovol (1893–1991). It comprises two sections: the sculpture collection, with artefacts from pre-Roman times through to the 20th century; and the 'Sentimental Museum', portraying daily life from the 15th to the 20th centuries through an extraordinary array of curios and household objects. Entrance to the museum is via a beautiful medieval courtyard garden, once part of the Royal Palace of the Kings and Queens of Catalonia and Aragon.
ⓐ Pl. Sant Iu 5–6 ① 933 105 800 ⓦ www.museumares.bcn.es
ⓔ museumares@mail.bcn.es ① 10.00–19.00 Tues–Sat,
10.00–15.00 Sun ⓝ Metro: Jaume I. Admission charge

RETAIL THERAPY

There are plenty of shops to choose from here, from the fashion boutiques of stylish Avinguda del Portal de l'Angel, a busy pedestrian thoroughfare, to the more old-fashioned specialist stores of the Barri Gotic. Here too, La Boqueria market (see page 68) is the best of over 40 food markets in town, and a must-see, even if you're not hungry.

ANTIQUES, BOOKS & MUSIC

Angel Batlle This antiquarian bookshop contains a fascinating collection of old maps, prints and nautical charts. ⓐ C/ Palla 23
① 933 015 884 ⓝ Metro: Liceu

L'Arca de l'Àvia A treasure trove of antique cottons, linens and silks.
ⓐ C/ Banys Nous 20 ① 933 021 598 ⓝ Metro: Liceu

Artur Ramon Anticuario Browse the paintings, furniture and valuable *objets d'art* in Barcelona's best antique store. ❸ C/ de la Palla 25 ❶ 933 025 970 Ⓝ Metro: Jaume I

Casa Beethoven Specialist music shop with an impressive stock of scores and sheet music, especially by Spanish and Catalan composers. ❸ La Rambla 97 ❶ 933 014 826 Ⓝ Metro: Liceu

ARTS & CRAFTS

Art Escudellers Glass and ceramic ware that is largely handmade by Spanish artisans and displayed by region. ❸ C/ Escudellers 23-25 ❶ 934 126 801 Ⓦ www.escudellers-art.com Ⓝ Metro: Liceu

La Manual Alpargatera An old-fashioned shop producing all manner of straw-woven items, including handmade traditional *espardenyes* (espadrilles) with esparto soles. ❸ C/ Avinyó 7 ❶ 933 010 172 Ⓝ Metro: Jaume I

🔺 *La Boqueria, a showcase for Catalan gastronomy*

Sala Parés Barcelona's top gallery, which once held an exhibition by the young Picasso, specialises in 19th- and 20th-century artworks. C/ Petritxol 5 933 187 020 Metro: Catalunya

FASHION

Mango Cheap, trendy designs for young fashionistas. C/ Portal de l'Àngel 933 176 985 www.mango.com Metro: Catalunya

Zara High-street fashion for men, women and children. C/ Portal de l'Àngel 32-34 933 010 898 www.zara.com Metro: Catalunya

FOOD

Mercat de la Boqueria Barcelona's main covered market is a veritable showcase for Catalan gastronomy, from fruit, herbs and vegetables to meat, fish and crustaceans. The cavernous market hall is best entered through an impressive wrought-iron gateway off La Rambla. Inside it's a riot of noise and activity, as market sellers, local shoppers, restaurateurs and tourists all jostle for the best buys of the day. It is an excellent place to stock up for a picnic or simply to soak up the flavours, colours and fragrances. La Rambla 100 933 182 017 07.00–20.00 Mon–Sat, closed Sun Metro: Liceu

MISCELLANEOUS

Cereria Subira The city's oldest shop, founded in 1761, sells a staggering variety of candles. Baixada Llibreteria 7 933 152 606 Metro: Jaume I

El Ingenio Come to this old-fashioned magic shop for fancy dress, tricks, games and carnival masks. C/ Rauric 6–8 933 177 138 Metro: Jaume I

TAKING A BREAK

Bar del Pi £ ❶ This pint-sized bar serves delicious coffee and a small selection of tapas alfresco. ❸ Pl. Sant Josep Oriol 1 ❶ 933 022 123 ● 09.00–23.00 Tues-Sun Ⓜ Metro: Liceu

La Clandestina £ ❷ New age tea house with juices, lassis and homemade cakes and pastries. Look out for the trapeze acts overhead. ❸ Baixada Viladecols 2 ❶ 933 190 533 ● 10.00–22.00 Ⓜ Metro: Jaume I

La Granja £ ❸ A classic milk bar with antique décor (there's even a section of Roman wall at the back) specialising in gloopy hot chocolate – try the spicy version with chilli. ❸ C/ Banys Nous 4 ❶ 933 026 975 ● 09.30–14.00, 16.00–21.00 Mon–Sat, 17.00–22.00 Sun Ⓜ Metro: Liceu

Milk £ ❹ This laid-back, baroque-style bar café serves up great cocktails and light snacks along with a popular Sunday brunch of smoothies and pancakes. ❸ C/ Gignas 21 ❶ 932 680 922 Ⓦ www.milkbarcelona.com ● 18.30–03.00 Mon-Sat, 12.00–03.00 Sun Ⓜ Metro: Jaume I

AFTER DARK

RESTAURANTS
Avoid La Rambla's overpriced restaurants and head into the narrow alleys and atmospheric squares of the Barri Gòtic.

Can Culleretes £ ❺ Enjoy robust country-style Catalan cuisine in an atmospheric, rustic setting in one of the city's oldest restaurants. Game is a speciality in season. ❸ C/ d'en Quintana 5 ❶ 933 176 485 ● 13.30–16.00, 21.00–23.00 Tue–Sat, 13.30–16.00 Sun Ⓜ Metro: Liceu

La Fonda £ ❻ A buzzy designer restaurant serving a good variety of stylish yet affordable Mediterranean dishes. ⓐ Passatge Escudellers 1 ❶ 933 017 515 ❷ 13.00–15.45 Ⓝ Metro: Liceu

Les Quinze Nits £ ❼ One of the Ciutat Vella's most popular restaurants. Ask for a table on the terrace overlooking the square, and tuck into a delicious seafood platter, paella or rabbit stew. Be prepared to queue. ⓐ Pl. Reial 5 ❶ 933 173 075 ❷13.00–15.45 Ⓝ Metro: Liceu

Cafè de l'Acadèmia ££ ❽ With a beautiful little terrace in a quiet church square, this is a wonderful place for a great set lunch or dinner of Catalan cooking with an innovative twist. ⓐ C/ Lleó 1 ❶ 933 198 253 ❷ 09.00–12.00, 13.30–17.00, 20.45–01.00 Mon–Fri, closed Sat & Sun Ⓝ Metro: Jaume I

Els Quatre Gats ££ ❾ Local artists and writers popularised this beautiful *Modernista* café in the early 1900s. Even the menu was designed by Picasso. Today the restaurant at the back serves simple Catalan staples. ⓐ C/ de Montsió 3 ❶ 933 024 140 ❷ 13.00–01.00 Ⓝ Metro: Catalunya

Pitarra ££ ❿ This old-fashioned restaurant, named after the 19th-century Catalan playwright, Frederic 'Pitarra' Soler, who once lived here, is known for its delicious paella. ⓐ C/ d'Avinyó 56 ❶ 933 011 647 ❷ 13.00–16.00, 20.30–23.00 Mon–Sat, closed Sun Ⓝ Metro: Liceu

Taxidermista ££ ⓫ A lively restaurant in an old taxidermist's studio, offering modern Mediterranean cuisine amid original cast-iron pillars and black-and-white marble floors. ⓐ Pl. Reial 8 ❶ 934 124 536 ❷ 13.30–16.00, 20.30–00.30 Tue–Sun, closed Mon Ⓝ Metro: Liceu

Neri Restaurant £££ ⓬ Stone Gothic arches, crushed velvet curtains and delicate Mediterranean dishes from Jordi Ruiz make for a perfect romantic dinner. ⓐ C/ Sant Sever 5 ⓣ 933 040 655 ⓦ www.hotelneri.com ⓛ 13.30–15.30, 20.30–23.00 ⓝ Metro: Jaume I

BARS & CLUBS

Café del Òpera The best café-bar on La Rambla – atmospheric, intimate and still with its original 19th-century décor. ⓐ La Rambla 74 ⓣ 93 302 41 80 ⓛ 08.30–02.15 ⓝ Metro: Liceu

Ginger A gem of a bar with hip jazzy sounds, deep yellow leather armchairs and a great range of cocktails and designer tapas. ⓐ C/ Palma de Sant Just 1 ⓣ 933 105 309 ⓛ 19.00–02.30 Tues–Thur, 19.00–03.00 Fri & Sat, closed Sun ⓝ Metro: Jaume I

Harlem Jazz Club Small, atmospheric and a choice nightspot for live jazz and blues. ⓐ C/ Comtessa de Sobradiel 8 ⓣ 93 310 07 55 ⓛ 20.00–04.00 Tues–Sun, closed Mon ⓝ Metro: Jaume I

Jamboree A hugely popular venue for live blues, jazz, soul, funk and occasional hip-hop until midnight, when it becomes a funky dance club. The adjoining **Tarantos** bar develops from flamenco joint to lively salsa club as the night progresses. ⓐ Pl. Reial 17 ⓣ 933 191 789 ⓦ www.masimas.com/jamboree ⓛ 22.00–late ⓝ Metro: Liceu

ENTERTAINMENT

Gran Teatre del Liceu Barcelona's celebrated belle époque opera house (see page 65). ⓐ La Rambla 51–9 ⓣ 934 859 900 ⓦ www.liceubarcelona.com ⓝ Metro: Liceu

La Barceloneta, El Born & La Ribera

With so much to see and do in the old town, it is easy to forget that Barcelona is a seaside city, with its fine sandy beaches, marinas and the giant waterfront leisure complexes of the Parc del Fòrum and the Maremàgnum. La Ribera (The Waterfront) was the medieval city's thriving maritime and trading district. In the 10th century, a settlement grew up here along what was then the seashore. Nowadays, it is a smart, in-vogue *barri* (quarter), brimming with trendy boutiques and sophisticated bars and restaurants.

The atmospheric neighbouring district of La Barceloneta was constructed on a triangular wedge of reclaimed land in the mid-18th century. With its narrow streets and ramshackle houses, over the centuries it has retained all the charm of an old Mediterranean fishing village, although it is now in the process of gentrification. It boasts some of the finest seafood restaurants in town.

SIGHTS & ATTRACTIONS

L'Aquàrium de Barcelona (Barcelona Aquarium)

Barcelona's ultra-modern Aquarium houses Europe's most important collection of Mediterranean marine life, with over 10,000 exotic sea creatures. The highlight is the 80 m (260 ft) glass tunnel, called the Oceanari, where a moving conveyor belt passes underneath sharks, sting rays, moonfish and other multicoloured species. ⓐ Moll d'Espanya ⓘ 932 217 474 ⓦ www.aquariumbcn.com ⓛ 09.30–21.00 ⓜ Metro: Drassanes or Barceloneta. Admission charge

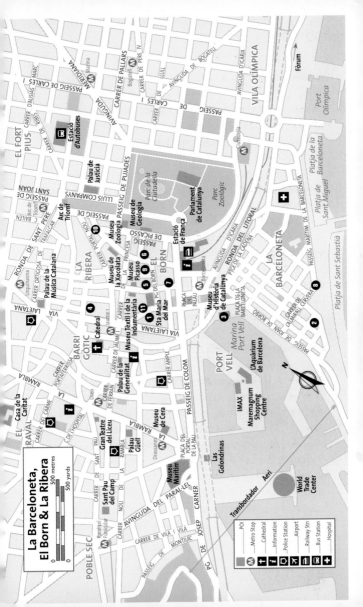

La Barceloneta

The quaint old district of La Barceloneta (Little Barcelona) was traditionally the home of seamen and port workers, and the clock tower on the Moll de la Barceloneta was once a lighthouse. Although the area has been greatly gentrified in recent years, the criss-cross grid of ancient narrow streets still holds children playing football while locals sit and chat, their washing fluttering overhead on the wrought-iron balconies. The heart of the district is the **Plaça de la Barceloneta**, with the beautiful baroque church of Sant Miquel del Port (Barceloneta's patron saint) and the newly rebuilt municipal market in the enormous central square of Plaça Poeta Boscà.

Ⓜ Metro: Barceloneta

Beaches

Barcelona's beaches offer bathers and sun-worshippers some of the cleanest city sea-bathing in the Mediterranean, with nearly 5 km (3 miles) of broad, sandy beaches stretching from La Barceloneta northwards. Facilities include some disabled access, lifeguards, public toilets, showers, beach bars known as xiringuitos, shops and restaurants. The three beaches nearest the city – Platjes Sant Miquel, Sant Sebastià and Barceloneta – get very crowded on hot days, so it is worth heading further north, off Avinguda del Litoral, to Platjes Nova Icària, Bogatell, Mar Bella (a nudist beach) or Nova Mar Bella, where there are windsurfers and small craft for hire during summer months.

The city has even created a new beach, Llevant, at the northernmost end of the city limits, which is very quiet although it does suffer from an ugly backdrop of high-rise apartment blocks. The most central beaches are fringed by the Passeig Marítim – the palm-lined boardwalk linking La Barceloneta to La Vila Olímpica, the 'twin towers' of Hotel Arts and the Mapfre building, signposted by Frank Gehry's glittering

copper *Fish* sculpture – the city's maritime symbol.
 Metro: Barceloneta, Ciutadella or Bogatell

El Born (The Born)
The tiny 'Born' district has recently emerged as one of the trendier
quarters of town, buzzing by day with funky shops, galleries and

⬥ *Stroll along the quayside in La Barceloneta*

craft workshops, and with fashionable bars and restaurants by night. Its main thoroughfare is the **Passeig del Born**. The name of this avenue means 'to joust' and for many centuries from the Middle Ages onwards, it was the scene of many city festivals, processions, tournaments, fairs, markets and carnivals. During the Inquisition, heretics were burned here. Today it plays host to a number of popular cafés and restaurants.

One end of the Passeig is dominated by the imposing church of Santa Maria del Mar (see page 79). At the other end, the old **Mercat del Born** (Born Market) – a glass and wrought-iron structure from the 1870s – is a magnificent example of 19th-century industrial architecture. Until 1971, it housed the city's main wholesale food market. Then, in 2001, some of the most extensive medieval archaeological remains in Europe were discovered here. The plan is to convert the building into the city's central library.
🅝 Metro: Barceloneta or Jaume I

Fòrum

Built for the six-month symposium known as the 2004 Forum of Cultures, this vast business and leisure complex transformed a large swathe of post-industrial wasteland by the sea. The landmark building is the Edifici Fòrum by Herzog and DeMeuron (who designed London's Tate Modern), a horizontal blue triangle covered in flowing water. The nearby Parc Diagonal Mar was designed by Enric Miralles (who designed the Scottish Parliament Building) and contains a bizarre angular lake and twirling aluminium tubing. Other features include a lido where you can swim out to the Illa Pangea, an island 60 metres (200 ft) from the shore. The large open spaces now provide an excellent venue for music festivals such as Summercase and Primavera Sound. 🅝 Metro: El Maresme-Fòrum

Las Golondrinas

The best way to see the old harbour and port area is to climb aboard one of the tour boats called *golondrinas* (swallows). Harbour tours depart regularly in summer and once an hour on winter weekends; excursions to the Port Olímpic and the Forum operate several times a day during summer. ❸ Porta de la Pau ❶ 934 423 106 ⓦ www.lasgolondrinas.com ⓝ Metro: Drassanes

Parc de la Ciutadella (Citadel Park)

This large leafy park is the green lung of Barcelona. It takes its name from the mighty citadel that dominated the city in the 18th century. In its midst are a boating-lake, playgrounds, lawns, promenades, the Parc Zoològic (see below) and a showy fountain – the Font Monumental – which Gaudí contributed to as a student. Notable buildings include the arsenal of the former citadel and the Castell dels Tres Dragons (Three Dragons Castle), a striking *Modernista* building that contains the Museu de Ciènces Naturals (Museum of Natural Science). ❸ Museu de Ciènces Naturals: Parc de la Ciutadella ❶ 933 196 912 ⓦ www.bcn.es/museuciences ❶ 10.00– 14.30 Tues & Wed, Fri–Sun, 10.00–18.30 Thur ⓝ Metro: Barceloneta

Parc Zoològic (Zoo)

Spain's leading zoo, with over 7,500 animals of 400 different species from all over the world, is always a popular outing with children, especially the under-fives who love the petting farm, the mini-train and the splashy shows of the dolphinarium. ❸ Parc de la Ciutadella ❶ 932 256 780 ⓦ www.zoobarcelona.com ❶ 10.00–17.00 (until 18.00 Mar–May, Oct; until 19.00 June–Sept) ⓝ Metro: Ciutadella. Admission charge

Port Vell (Old Port)

No other single Olympic project changed the face of the city as dramatically as the construction of Port Vell. This former industrial area of ships and sprawling warehouses has undergone a massive transformation and is now a popular recreation area, with an aquarium, a cinema complex and Maremàgnum (ⓦ www.maremagnum.es), a huge shopping centre with cafés, bars and restaurants. Approach it via the Rambla de Mar, a series of undulating wooden walkways and wavelike metal arches, which stretches out over the sea like a watery extension of La Rambla (see page 58). Ⓝ Metro: Drassanes

● *Street sculpture – Gambrinus by Xavier Mariscal*

Santa Maria del Mar (Holy Mary of the Sea)

The magnificent Gothic Basilica of Santa Maria del Mar is arguably
Barcelona's finest church, striking in its simplicity. It lies at the
heart of La Ribera. The original settlement grew up around a tiny
10th-century chapel here called Santa Maria de les Arenes (Holy
Mary of the Sands), built on what was then the seashore. During
the 14th century, it was transformed into today's imposing 'seaside
church' as a show of the city's maritime power. The foundation
stone commemorates the Catalan conquest of Sardinia.

The plain façade belies a majestic spacious interior of slim
octagonal columns and narrow lofty naves. The church is surprisingly
lacking in ornamentation, as most of its treasures were lost during
the Spanish Civil War. However, the 15th-century ship atop the altar
serves as a reminder of the city's seafaring heyday. ⓐ Passeig del Born 1
ⓘ 933 102 390 ⓛ 09.00–13.30, 16.30–20.00 ⓝ Metro: Barceloneta

CULTURE

Museu de la Xocolata (Chocolate Museum)

A paradise for chocaholics, this attractive museum houses a fabulous
collection of *mones* (elaborate chocolate sculptures) made by
Barcelona's master chefs for the yearly Easter competition. The
mones range from a hulking model of Floquet de Neu, the Zoo's
deceased albino gorilla, to the windmill scene from Don Quijote or
the chariot race from Ben Hur. There is also a brief history of cocoa
and chocolate, a glass-fronted cookery workshop and, naturally,
a wonderful chocolate shop. ⓐ C/ Comerç 36 ⓘ 932 687 878
ⓦ www.museuxocolata.com ⓛ 10.00–19.00 Mon, Wed–Sat,
10.00–15.00 Sun ⓝ Metro: Jaume I. Admission charge

Museu d'Història de Catalunya (History Museum of Catalonia)

The Palau de Mar (Palace of the Sea), the port's old general warehouse, is a fine example of 19th-century industrial architecture. Nowadays, it contains the History Museum of Catalonia, a fascinating hands-on museum illustrating the great moments of the region's history and providing a valuable insight into Catalan lifestyle over the centuries. The museum café, on the top floor of the Palau de Mar, offers one of the best views of the city. ➌ Palau de Mar, Pl. Pau Vila 3 ❶ 932 254 700 ⓦ www.mhcat.net ⓛ 10.00–20.00 Tues, 10.00–19.00 Wed–Sat, 10.00–14.30 Sun ⓝ Metro: Barceloneta. Admission charge

Museu Picasso

Not only is this museum the city's greatest tourist attraction, but it is also the most important and most complete collection of early artworks by Pablo Picasso in the world. Although the great Spanish artist was born in Andalucía, he moved to Barcelona in 1895, when he was just 14 years old, and spent seven of his most formative years here.

The outstanding collection is housed in five adjoining medieval palaces on the beautiful Carrer Montcada. It traces Picasso's career from 1890 to 1904, from early childhood sketches and a range of styles from his time at La Lotja art school to the famous Blue Period. The collection then leaps to 1917 and the more mature, distinctive Cubism of later years, and demonstrates his versatility and extraordinary artistic development over the decades.
➊ C/ Montcada 15–23 ❶ 933 196 310 ⓦ www.museupicasso.bcn.es
ⓛ 10.00–20.00 Tues–Sun ⓝ Metro: Jaume I. Admission charge

Museu Tèxtil i de la Indumentària (Textile and Clothing Museum)

This delightful museum is housed in a beautiful 14th-century palace on one of Barcelona's most aristocratic streets. It illustrates how the city rose to prosperity during the 1800s, thanks to its thriving textile industry, with sumptuous displays of tapestries, textiles, lace, clothing and accessories dating from medieval to modern times. C/ Montcada 12–14 933 104 516 www.museutextil.bcn.es 10.00–18.00 Tues–Sat, 10.00–15.00 Sun Metro: Jaume I. Admission charge

Palau de la Música Catalana (Palace of Catalan Music)

This dazzling palace, built in the pure *Modernista* style by Domenech i Montaner in 1908, is considered one of the finest concert houses in the world. Each year it hosts some 300 concerts, with an attendance of over half a million people. In a city full of architectural wonders, it stands out as one of the greatest works of Modernism and a symbol of the renaissance of Catalan culture. Indeed, in 1997 UNESCO declared it a World Heritage Site. If you have time, go to a concert – it's the best way to enjoy the building. C/ de Sant Francesc de Paula 2 932 681 000 http://home.palaumusica.org 10.00–15.30 Metro: Urquinaona

RETAIL THERAPY

ART & DESIGN

Galeria Maeght A prestigious gallery of 20th-century art, design and photography. C/ Montcada 25 (1st floor) 933 014 245 Metro: Jaume I

Museu Picasso An excellent museum shop, brimming with Picasso-inspired souvenirs and gifts. C/ Montcada 15 933 196 310 www.museupicasso.bcn.es Metro: Jaume I

FASHION & ACCESSORIES

Alea Majoral Galería de Joyas Tiny boutique at the heart of La Ribera, showcasing up-and-coming Catalan jewellers. ⓐ C/ Argenteria 66 ⓣ 933 101 373 Ⓜ Metro: Jaume I or Barceloneta

Maremàgnum A huge waterfront leisure complex with numerous fashion boutiques including Calvin Klein, Mango, H&M, Quiksilver, Women's Secret and top Spanish designer, Adolfo Domínguez. ⓐ Maremàgnum, Moll d'Espanya ⓣ 932 258 100 Ⓦ www.maremagnum.es Ⓜ Metro: Barceloneta or Drassanes

On Land The quintessential Born boutique with a smattering of sharp and sexy streetwear from local fashion heroes such as Josep Font or Divinas Palabras. ⓐ C/ Princesa 25 ⓣ 933 101 211 Ⓦ www.on-land.com Ⓜ Metro: Jaume I

⬤ *Frank Gehry's* Fish *sculpture outside the Hotel Arts on the seafront*

TAKING A BREAK

Bubó £ ❶ Carles Mampel's sumptuous and intricately designed pralines, sachertortes and petits fours make for a seriously classy afternoon coffee. For savoury treats there's a tiny tapas bar next door. ⓐ C/ Caputxes 10 ❶ 932 687 221 Ⓦ www.bubo.ws ❶ 15.00–22.00 Mon, 10.00–22.00 Tues, Wed, Sun, 10.00–23.00 Thur, 10.00–01.00 Fri & Sat Ⓝ Metro: Jaume I

Daguiri £ ❷ A cheery and very laid-back seafront terrace café with WiFi, a raft of international newspapers, and a range of juices, salads and homemade cakes. ⓐ C/ Grau i Tores 59 ❶ 932 215 109 ❶ 11.00–02.00 Mon-Fri & Sun, 10.00–01.00 Sat, June–Oct; 11.00–02.00 Mon, Thur–Sun, Nov–May Ⓝ Metro: Barceloneta

La Miranda del Museu £ ❸ You don't need to buy a ticket to the museum to enjoy this little-known rooftop café and restaurant with the most spectacular views over the port. Perfect for a coffee break on the terrace or a good value set lunch. ⓐ Museu d'Història de Catalunya, Pl. Pau Vila 3 ❶ 932 255 007 ❶ 10.00–19.00 Tues & Wed, 10.00–19.00, 21.00–23.00 Thur–Sat, closed Sun Ⓝ Metro: Barceloneta

AFTER DARK

RESTAURANTS

Most people head to La Barceloneta to eat in its smart harbourside seafood restaurants – a prime location for paella and people-watching – while El Born and La Ribera are packed with fashionable bistros and brasseries.

Cuines Santa Caterina £ ④ Set in the flashy new Santa Caterina market, this huge airy restaurant with wooden refectory-style tables serves up international fusion dishes, from tempura to traditional Catalan botifarra sausage. ⓐ Mercat Santa Caterina, Av. Francesc Cambó ⓣ 932 689 918 ⓛ 13.00–16.00, 20.00–23.15 Mon–Wed & Sun, 13.00–16.00, 20.00–00.15 Thur–Sat ⓝ Metro: Jaume I

Euskal Etxea £ ⑤ The best place in Barcelona to try pintxos (the Basque version of tapas), with an open buffet of exquisite little snacks speared on a slice of bread. The restaurant at the back serves heartier Basque specialities. ⓐ Placeta Montcada 1–3 ⓣ 933 102 185 ⓛ Bar: 18.30–23.30 Mon, 11.30–16.00 18.30–23.30 Tues–Sat. Restaurant: 20.30–23.30 Mon 13.30–16.00 20.30–23.30 Tues–Sat. Closed Sun ⓝ Metro: Jaume I

La Paradeta £ ⑥ Excellent value seafood served up canteen style: queue to choose from piles of fresh clams, shrimp and fish on ice, tell them how you want it cooked and wait for your number to be called. ⓐ C/ Comercial 7 ⓣ 932 681 939 ⓛ 20.00–23.30 Tues–Fri, 13.00–16.00, 20.00–00.00 Sat, 13.00–16.00 Sun ⓝ Metro: Arc de Triomf

Cal Pep ££ ⑦ A classic locals' restaurant specialising in seafood. Sit at the bar and try some of the mouth-watering tapas. ⓐ Pl. de les Olles 8 ⓣ 933 107 961 ⓛ 20.00–23.45 Mon, 13.30–16.00, 20.00–23.45 Tues–Sat. Closed Sun ⓦ www.calpep.com ⓝ Metro: Barceloneta or Jaume I

Can Majó ££ ⑧ One of Barceloneta's top seafood restaurants serves up paella and piles of fresh lobster and langoustines just a stone's throw from the beach. Book in advance for Sunday lunchtime. ⓐ C/ Almirall Aixada 23 ⓣ 932 215 455 ⓛ 13.00–16.00, 20.00–23.30 Tues–Sat, 13.00–16.00 Sun ⓝ Metro: Barceloneta

ABAC £££ ❾ Michelin-starred chef Xavier Pellicier serves exceptional Spanish haute cuisine in this elegant minimalist restaurant.
🄰 C/ Rec 79–89 🄣 933 196 600 🅦 www.restaurantabac.com
🄻 20.30–22.30 Mon, 13.30–15.30, 20.30–22.30 Tues–Sat,
closed Mon lunch & Sun 🄽 Metro: Barceloneta

Comerç 24 £££ ❿ Avant-garde Catalan cuisine from Carles Abellan, a protégé of Ferran Adrià. Enjoy a parade of tiny, eccentric dishes in sharp and sexy surroundings. 🄰 C/ Comerç 24 🄣 933 192 102
🅦 www.comerc24.com 🄻 13.30–15.30, 20.30–00.00 Mon–Sat.
Closed Sun 🄽 Metro: Arc de Triomf

Hofmann £££ ⓫ Spain's top cookery school and the eponymous restaurant of celebrity chef Mey Hofmann. Expect clever playful dishes with especially interesting desserts such as a fruit pudding presented in an edible spun sugar jam jar. 🄰 C/ Argenteria 74–8
🄣 933 195 889 🅦 www.hofmann-bcn.com 🄻 13.30–15.30,
21.00–23.15 Mon–Fri, closed Sat & Sun 🄽 Metro: Jaume I

BARS & CLUBS
CDLC The dance floor at Carpe Diem Lounge Club is surrounded by veiled white beds where the VIPs of Barcelona drink their expensive cocktails and try to spot all the other celebrities. 🄰 Passeig Marítim 32
🄣 932 240 470 🅦 www.cdlcbarcelona.com 🄻 22.00–02.30 Mon–Wed,
12.00–03.00 Thur–Sun 🄽 Metro: Ciutadella-Vila Olímpica

Club Catwalk Right under the glamorous Hotel Arts, this swish club is where all the aspiring models go to preen and dance to R&B, house and hip-hop. 🄰 C/ Ramon Trias Fargas 🄣 932 216 161 🅦 www.clubcatwalk.net
🄻 00.00–05.30 Wed–Sun 🄽 Metro: Ciutadela-Vila Olímpica

Le Kasbah An intimate Moroccan-style bar playing easy listening, minimal, house, funk, latin and jazz sounds. ⓐ Palau del Mar, Pl. Pau Vilà ⓣ 932 380 722 ⓦ www.ottozutz.com ⓛ 22.30–03.00 ⓝ Metro: Barceloneta

Razzmatazz Five different dance floors under one roof, each with different music genres and some of the city's top DJs. ⓐ C/ Almogavers 122 ⓦ www.salarazzmatazz.com ⓛ 01.00–05.00 Fri & Sat. Closed Sun–Thur ⓝ Metro: Marina

El Xampanyet A tiny champagne bar with blue-tiled walls, marble tables and a zinc bar, combining old-fashioned charm with a lively, young crowd. ⓐ C/ Montcada 22 ⓣ 933 197 003 ⓛ 12.00–16.00, 19.00–23.30 Tues–Sat, 12.00–16.00 Sun, closed Mon ⓝ Metro: Jaume I

CINEMA
IMAX Port Vell Think big with this giant wraparound 3-D screen. ⓐ C/ Moll d'Espanya ⓣ 932 351 111 ⓦ www.imaxportvell.com ⓝ Metro: Drassanes

Yelmo Icària Cineplex The 15 screens offer Hollywood blockbusters and mainstream Spanish releases, all in the original version with subtitles in Spanish. ⓐ C/ Salvador Espriú 61 ⓣ 93 2 217 585 ⓦ www.yelmocineplex.com ⓝ Metro: Ciutadella-Vila Olímpica

ENTERTAINMENT
This area contains two of the city's main concert venues. There are also occasional concerts and recitals in the Basilica of Santa Maria del Mar (see page 79), and open-air theatre, concerts and dance events in Parc de la Ciutadella (see page 77) during summer.

L'Auditori This modern arts complex is home to the National Catalan Orchestra. The Sala Simfònica stages full orchestral concerts, while the more intimate Sala Polivante is popular for recitals and chamber ensembles. After night performances, the Arts Bus runs concert-goers to Plaça de Catalunya. ⓐ C/ Lepant 150 ⓣ 932 479 300 ⓦ www.auditori.org Ⓜ Metro: Marina

Palau de la Música Catalana (Palace of Catalan Music) Undoubtedly the most spectacular venue for classical music in town, staging frequent concerts by the Cor de Cambra (Chamber Choir) del Palau de la Música, or by the amateur Orfeó Català choir, for whom the auditorium was originally built (see page 81). ⓐ C/ Sant Francesc de Paula 2 ⓣ 932 681 000 ⓦ http://home.palaumusica.org Ⓜ Metro: Urquinaona

⬤ The spectacular Palau de la Música Catalana

L'Eixample & Gràcia

L'Eixample (The Extension) was built between 1860 and 1920 to accommodate the burgeoning bourgeois population, and to merge the outlying villages of Sants, Sarrià-Sant Gervasi and Gràcia into the modern city. Its construction coincided with the emergence of Catalan *Modernisme*, and many of its wealthy new residents commissioned the great architects of the day to design grand mansions for them in this flamboyant new style. As a consequence, the district resembles a huge open-air museum, containing most of the city's greatest *Modernista* landmarks, including Gaudí's legendary Sagrada Família church, Casa Batlló and La Pedrera. Today the Eixample remains a wealthy district, brimming with designer boutiques, smart hotels, sophisticated bars and restaurants.

To the north, the 'village' of Gràcia has long been known as a radical centre of Catalanism and, despite being completely engulfed by the city these days, the district still maintains a village atmosphere and the locals consider themselves Graciencs rather than Barcelonans.

CERDÀ'S EIXAMPLE

Ildefons Cerdà's geometric grid design for the Eixample was an innovative plan in its day, which broke completely with former models of Spanish urban planning. It divided the city into 550 symmetrical blocks covering an area of 23 sq km (9 sq miles), with the aptly named Avinguda Diagonal cutting through the blocks at a 45° angle to add a touch of quirkiness.

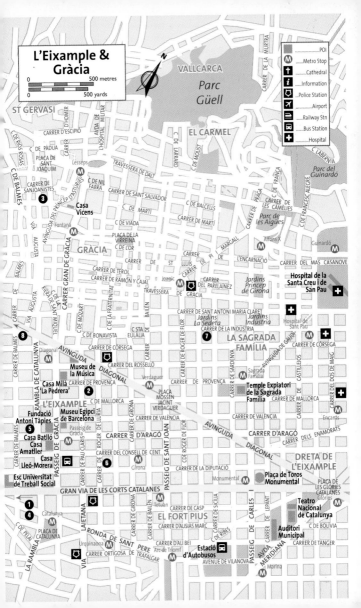

L'Eixample & Gràcia

0 ____ 500 metres
0 ____ 500 yards

VALLCARCA

Parc Güell

EL CARMEL

ST GERVASI

PLAÇA DE SANT JOAQUIM

Lesseps

TRAVESSERA DE DALT

Casa Vicens

GRÀCIA

Parc de les Aigües

Alfons X

L'ENCARNACIÓ

Jardins Príncep de Girona

Hospital de la Santa Creu i de San Pau

Jardins La Sedeta

Jardins Industria

LA SAGRADA FAMÍLIA

Museu de la Música

Casa Milà 'La Pedrera'

L'EIXAMPLE

Temple Expiatori de la Sagrada Família

Fundació Antoni Tàpies

Museu Egipci de Barcelona

Casa Batlló

Casa Amatller

Casa Lleó-Morera

Esc Universitat de Treball Social

DRETA DE L'EIXAMPLE

Plaça de Toros Monumental

GRAN VIA DE LES CORTS CATALANES

PLAÇA DE LES GLÒRIES CATALANES

Teatro Nacional de Catalunya

EL FORT PIUS

Auditori Municipal

PLAÇA DE CATALUNYA

Estació d'Autobusos

Parc del Guinardó

Legend

- POI
- Metro Stop
- Cathedral
- Information
- Police Station
- Airport
- Railway Stn
- Bus Station
- Hospital

SIGHTS & ATTRACTIONS

Casa Milà – 'La Pedrera' (Milà House – 'The Stone Quarry')

Gaudí was at the peak of his architectural career when he constructed the extraordinary apartment block of Casa Milà for dilettante politician Pere Milà in 1912. It was Gaudí's last and most famous secular building, and also one of his most inventive – a triumph of aesthetics over practicality, built entirely on columns and arches, with sinuous lines and rippling limestone façades, supposedly without a single straight line or right-angled corner. Every last detail is intricately designed, right down to the crooked banisters, ergonomic doorknobs, balconies of recycled wrought-ironwork and ceramic-encrusted chimneys of the roof terrace.

Sadly, soon after its construction, Casa Milà was to become Spain's most controversial apartment block. Its innovative appearance so shocked Barcelonans when it was built that they nicknamed it 'La Pedrera' ('The Stone Quarry'). After years of neglect, it was eventually declared a World Heritage Site by UNESCO in 1984 (the first 20th-century building to achieve the honour) and, ironically, it is now one of the city's most admired buildings.

Inside the building is the fascinating Espai Gaudí, an exhibition about the origins and construction of Casa Milà, with drawings, models, photographs and audiovisuals. But the highlight of any visit is undoubtedly the extraordinary undulating roof with its strangely shaped chimney stacks and amazing bird's-eye vistas of the Eixample. During summer weekends, the roof terrace is the spectacular venue for *La Pedrera de Nit*, a series of open-air evening concerts.

ⓐ Passeig de Gràcia 92 ⓣ 902 400 973 ⓛ 10.00–20.00
Ⓜ Metro: Diagonal. Admission charge

⬤ Modernista *architecture in L'Eixample*

Hospital de la Santa Creu i de San Pau

This beautiful unusual hospital complex forms one of Europe's finest ensembles of Modernism, designed by the innovative architect Domènech i Montaner. Not only did he defy the orderliness of the Eixample by aligning the buildings at 45° to the street grid, but he also broke with the tradition of having one large hospital building, by creating a 'hospital-village' of 18 small pavilions, connected by a series of underground passages. Construction began in 1902 and, when the hospital was eventually inaugurated in 1930, it was considered to be

LA MANZANA DE LA DISCORDIA

The most impressive block on the Passeig de Gràcia (between Carrer d'Aragó and Carrer Consell de Cent) is called the Manzana de la Discordia (Block of Discord), because of the clashing architectural styles of Casa Amatller, Casa Batlló and Casa Lleó-Morera (see below) – three of the most celebrated architectural ensembles and a magnificent showcase for the city's greatest exponents of *Modernisme*, Montaner, Cadafalch and Gaudí. View them by day and by night, when their façades are magically lit.

one of the most advanced in Europe. It ceased to function as a working hospital in 2006 due to the demands of modern-day medicine and is now mainly used for research, although it may eventually become a museum of *Modernisme*. The entire complex is protected as a UNESCO World Heritage Site. ❸ C/ de Sant Antoni María Claret 167 ❶ 932 919 000 ❿ www.santpau.es ⓝ Metro: Hospital de Sant Pau

La Manzana de Discordia

The most celebrated city block or *manzana* ('apple', named after the round shape of the blocks in the Eixample, due to their chamfered corners) of 'discord' contains three clashing *Modernista* masterpieces. Heading uphill towards Tibidabo, the first is the white, neo-Gothic wedding cake fantasy of the Casa Lleó Morera (1902-5) by Lluís Domènech i Montaner. It stands out for its sumptuous stonework and cupola. At number 41 stands the Casa Amatller (1900), designed by Josep Puig i Cadfalch for a local chocolate magnate; look out for the unusual stepped Flemish gable and cheeky stone figures carved around the doorway. The building currently houses the Centre del Modernisme, which provides information and multilingual guides on the Ruta del Modernisme (see page 20). The most photographed of them all is next door at number 43: Antoni Gaudí's masterful Casa Batlló (1907), whose sinuous curves stand in stark contrast to its geometric neighbour. The dazzling polychrome façade, tibia-like stone columns and humped scaly roof are said to represent the triumph of St George over the dragon (see page 12). An audio-guided tour of the extraordinary interior, and the rooftop with its unique

⬥ *Rooftop chimneys at Casa Milà 'La Pedrera'*

chimneys, reveals Gaudí's unparalleled freedom of imagination and abstract genius. ⓐ Passeig de Gràcia 35–43, Casa Batlló 43 ⓣ 932 160 306 ⓦ www.casabatllo.es ⓝ 09.00–20.00 ⓜ Metro: Passeig de Gràcia

Parc Güell

The wealthy Güell family commissioned a number of works from Antoni Gaudí over the years, including Palau Güell (see page 107) and this eccentric hilltop park high up above the district of Gràcia. Sadly, Eusebi Güell's plan to create a residential garden city here, with 60 houses set in formal gardens, never came to fruition and the park was deemed a failure in its day. Only two houses were built, including the one where Gaudí briefly lived (now the Casa Museu Gaudí, containing a small but moving selection of his personal artefacts, wrought-ironwork and items of furniture).

Today, Parc Güell is considered one of the city's treasures, outstanding for its clever fusion of architectural elements into the landscaping. In 1969, it was declared a national monument. Throughout its 20 hectares (49 acres), there are surreal sculptures, steps, bridges, and paths raised on columns of 'dripping' stonework. The main entrance is especially impressive, with massive wrought-iron gates, flanked by two oval pavilions with colourful mosaic domes. From here, a grand stairway, ornamented by a mosaic salamander fountain, leads to the Sala Hipòstila, a vast cavernous space originally intended as the marketplace. Its circular rooftop plaza, supported by 86 fluted columns, is edged with a curved continuous bench covered in multi-coloured *trencadís* (broken ceramics). The plaza affords far-reaching city vistas and makes an ideal picnic spot. ⓐ C/ d'Olot (park); Carretera del Carmel (museum) ⓣ 932 130 488 (park); 932 193 811 (museum) ⓛ Museum: 10.00–18.00 Oct–Mar; 10.00–19.00 Apr–Sept ⓝ Bus 24 Metro: Vallcarca (then 10-minute walk)

Passeig de Gràcia

This broad leafy boulevard forms the axis of Cerdà's plan for the Eixample (see feature box on page 88) and is considered to be the 'Champs-Élysées of Catalonia'. It was constructed in 1827 on the path that once joined Barcelona to the village of Gràcia, and today its central tree-lined pedestrian walkway forms a northern extension of La Rambla (see page 58). By the turn of the 20th century, it was one of the most sought-after residential streets, flanked by some of the city's most elegant and striking mansions. Other special features

● *Tip-top detail at La Sagrada Família*

include the unusual Gaudíesque 'bench and lamppost' ensembles. It was not until the 1920s that the boulevard became a major shopping thoroughfare. ❸ Passeig de Gràcia Ⓜ Metro: Passeig de Gràcia

Plaça de Catalunya

This busy square is the nerve-centre of Barcelona, at the confluence of many major thoroughfares: La Rambla and Avinguda del Portal de l'Angel to the south; Passeig de Gràcia and La Rambla de Catalunya to the north. The square adopted its final form in the 1920s, when an extensive esplanade joined the Old Town with the Eixample, and the square replaced Plaça de Sant Jaume as the heart of Barcelona. Today, with its sculptures and symmetrical fountains, it is a central meeting point for Barcelonans.

Temple Expiatori de la Sagrada Família (Expiatory Temple of the Holy Family)

This extraordinary building is surely the most unusual temple in the world, and Barcelona's most distinctive landmark. It also represents the synthesis of architectural genius Antoni Gaudí's work. The first stone was laid in 1882 and the devout Catholic worked on the project for over 40 years. Such was his commitment to the building, he even lived in an on-site workshop studio for the last 15 years of his life. His dream was to create Europe's biggest temple and a bible in stone, with three façades representing the birth, death and resurrection of Christ, and 18 mosaic-clad domes and pinnacles to symbolise the 12 Apostles, the four Evangelists, the Virgin Mary and Christ.

Following his untimely death in 1926 (see page 13), only the crypt, the majority of the Nativity façade, the apse and just four towers were complete, and his plans for the rest of the building were uncertain after blueprints were destroyed by anarchists in the Civil War. After his death, there was great controversy as to whether or not the work should resume. Since 1952 the Passion façade has been added and there are now eight completed towers, each over 100 m (325 ft) tall. There is a museum in the crypt, documenting the past, present and future of Gaudí's monumental, unfinished cathedral through photographs, plans, audiovisuals and original sketches, together with decorative items and maquettes of his life's work in general.

The entrance ticket includes admission to the building work in progress, the museum and access to the multi-coloured towers, either on foot or by lift, for breathtaking views of the city. The Nativity façade – devoted to the birth and early life of Christ with three doors representing Faith, Hope and Charity – is best viewed from the small park in Plaça Gaudí. The detail of sculpture on the façade is truly extraordinary, depicting almost 100 species of plants and as many types of animals, including Gaudí's beloved chameleons, which can be seen carved into the stonework all over the cathedral. By contrast, the post-Gaudí Passion façade, completed in 1990 by sculptor Josep Maria Subirachs, is more angular, minimalist and contemporary, signifying the pain and sacrifice of the final part of Christ's life. The main façade of the basilica, devoted to the Celestial Glory, is now well under way.

It is estimated that there are a further 80 years of work, including the destruction of an entire block of apartments in front of the Glory façade to create an entrance avenue. Matters will not be speeded up by the subterranean construction of the AVE high-speed train line next to the temple. Nevertheless, the Sagrada Família remains one of the great architectural wonders of the world and a must-see for every visitor to the city. ⓐ Pl. de la Sagrada Família (temple); C/ Mallorca 401 (museum) ⓣ 932 073 031 ⓦ www.sagradafamilia.org ⓛ 09.00–18.00 Oct–Mar; 09.00–20.00 Apr–Sept ⓜ Metro: Sagrada Família. Admission charge

CULTURE

Fundació Antoni Tàpies (Antoni Tàpies Foundation)

Catalan artist Antoni Tàpies founded the Tàpies Foundation in 1984 to promote the study and understanding of modern art. It contains

⬭ *The curvaceous main entrance to Parc Güell*

a specialist library, which documents art and artists of the 20th century, and one of the most extensive collections of Tàpies' own paintings, drawings and sculptures. It also hosts temporary exhibitions of contemporary art and culture.

The Foundation is housed in a particularly unusual building, built in the 1880s by Lluís Domènech i Montaner, and it is considered to be the initiator of the Modernist movement. The imposing Mudéjar-style façade is crowned by the eye-catching wire sculpture *Cloud and Chair*, made by Tàpies in 1990, which has since become a symbol of the Foundation. ❸ C/ d'Aragó 255 ❶ 934 870 315 Ⓦ www.fundaciotapies.org 🕙 10.00–20.00 Tues–Sun Ⓜ Metro: Passeig de Gràcia. Admission charge

Museu de la Música (Music Museum)

The city music museum finally re-opened in spring 2007, after relocating from its previous home in the Palau del Baró de Quadras in 2001. Beautifully displayed in sleek, modern surroundings are some 500 instruments ranging from harps and violins to Lebanese derbekkahs and a full range of castanets and the Catalan flabiol (a type of recorder). There's a wealth of documents, such as letters from cellist Pau Casals and original sheet music by composer Enric Granados, sound recordings and even an interactive space where visitors can try out instruments for themselves. ❸ C/ Padilla 155 2nd floor ❶ 932 563 650 Ⓦ www.museumusica.bcn.cat 🕙 11.00–21.00 Mon, Wed–Fri, 10.00–19.00 Sat & Sun Ⓜ Metro: Glòries. Admission charge

Museu Egipci de Barcelona (Egyptian Museum of Barcelona)

An outstanding collection of artefacts from Ancient Egypt owned by Egyptologist and hotelier Jordi Clos. Exhibits include everything from copper mirrors to an amazingly intact 5,000-year-old bed, mummified animals, infant sarcophagi and the wonderful statue of Osiris breastfeeding her son Horus. Book ahead on Friday and Saturday nights to see dramatic reconstructions of themes such as the life of Cleopatra or the mummification ritual. ⓐ C/ València 284 ⓣ 934 880 188 ⓦ www.fundclos.com ⓛ 10.00–20.00 Mon–Sat, 10.00–14.00 Sun ⓝ Metro: Passeig de Gràcia. Admission charge

RETAIL THERAPY

ART & ANTIQUES
Bulevard dels Antiquaris A wonderful mall with some 70 shops specialising in oil paintings, jewellery, dolls, furniture and limited edition Tàpies and Miró prints. ⓐ Passeig de Gràcia 55 ⓣ 932 154 499 ⓦ www.bulevarddelsantiquaris.com ⓝ Metro: Passeig de Gràcia

FASHION
Adolfo Dominguez One of Spain's top menswear designers, famed for making linen suits popular with the slogan 'wrinkles are beautiful'. ⓐ Passeig de Gràcia 89 ⓣ 932 151 339 ⓦ www.adolfodominguez.com ⓝ Metro: Passeig de Gràcia

Antonio Miró A local designer, celebrated worldwide for his shoes, specs, furnishings and sombre fashions. ⓐ C/ Consell de Cent 349 ⓣ 934 870 670 ⓦ www.antoniomiro.es ⓝ Metro: Passeig de Gràcia

Bagués One of the world's leading Modernist jewellers, housed in Casa Amatller. ⓐ Passeig de Gràcia 41 ⓣ 932 160 174 ⓝ Metro: Passeig de Gràcia

Camper Catalonia's most famous footwear: colourful, almost childish designs in exquisitely soft leather with the trademark recycled soles. ⓐ C/ Pelai 13 ⓣ 933 024 124 ⓦ www.camper.com ⓝ Metro: Cataluyna

Muxart Fantastic creations by flamboyant Barcelonan shoe designer, Hermenegildo Muxart. ⓐ C/ Rosselló 230 ❶ 934 871 591 ⓦ www.muxart.com ⓝ Metro: Provença or Diagonal

GIFTS & DESIGN

Dos i Una Barcelona's first design shop is full of state-of-the-art gadgetry and amusing gift ideas. ⓐ C/ Rossello 275 ❶ 932 177 032 ⓝ Metro: Diagonal

Vinçon An über-trendy home design store in the beautiful *Modernista* mansion where artist Ramon Casas once lived. ⓐ Passeig de Gracià 96 ❶ 932 156 050 ⓦ www.vincon.com ⓝ Metro: Passeig de Gracià

TAKING A BREAK

Bodega Sepúlveda £ ❶ The speciality at this genuine locals' bar is *boquerons* (fresh anchovies). ⓐ C/ Sepúlveda 173 ❶ 932 359 44 ❶ Closed Sat morning & Sun ⓝ Metro: Universitat

Bar Mut ££ ❷ An upmarket bar that retains its original *Modernista* décor. Delectable seafood tapas are nibbled with a glass of the eponymous vermouth. ⓐ C/ Pau Claris 192 ❶ 932 174 338 ❶ 08.30–24.00 Mon–Fri, 10.30–24.00 Sat, 20.30–24.00 Sun ⓝ Metro: Diagonal

Flash-flash Tortilleria ££ ❸ *Tortillas* (omelettes) in 60 varieties and salads – perfect for a light lunch in monochrome seventies surroundings. ⓐ C/ Granada del Penedès 25 ❶ 932 370 990 ❶ 11.00–02.00 ⓝ Metro: Diagonal

Inopia ££ ❹ The latest tapas sensation comes from Albert Adrià, brother to the world-famous Ferran. There's no culinary trickery here though, just perfectly executed versions of classic tapas served in bright, modern décor. ⓐ C/ Tamarit 104 ⓣ 934 245 231 ⓛ 19.00–24.00 Mon–Fri, 13.00–15.30 19.00–24.00 Sat, closed Sun Ⓝ Metro: Poble Sec

AFTER DARK

RESTAURANTS

El Glop de la Rambla £ ❺ Popular, affordable restaurant serving char-grilled meat dishes and local wines. ⓐ Rambla Catalunya 65 ⓣ 934 870 097 ⓦ www.el-glop.com ⓛ 13.00–16.00 20.30–23.00 Mon–Fri, 20.30–23.00 Sat, closed Sat lunch & Sun Ⓝ Metro: Passeig de Gràcia

Noti ££ ❻ Creative Spanish-Italian cuisine in a sleek, urban interior – a popular choice for business lunches. ⓐ C/ Roger de Llúria 35 ⓣ 933 426 673 ⓦ www.noti-universal.com ⓛ 13.30–16.00, 20.30–24.00 Mon–Fri, 20.30–24.00 Sat, closed Sun Ⓝ Metro: Passeig de Gràcia

Alkimia £££ ❼ The Michelin star makes booking ahead essential but these gourmet versions of classic Spanish dishes are well worth the trouble. One of the most desirable tables in town. ⓐ C/ Indústria 79 ⓣ 932 076 115 ⓛ 13.30–15.30, 20.30–23.00 Mon–Fri, closed Sat & Sun Ⓝ Metro: Joanic

Saüc £££ ❽ An unmissable experience for anyone serious about food, the 'elderberry' has a surprisingly affordable set lunch and highly accomplished takes on Catalan classics. Book well ahead. ⓐ Passatge Lluis Pellicer 12 ⓣ 933 210 189 ⓛ 13.30–15.30, 20.30–22.30 Tues–Sat, closed Sun Ⓝ Metro: Hospital Clínic

BARS, CLUBS & LIVE MUSIC

Antilla BCN Latin Club The best salsateca in town has dance classes, live music concerts and the full range of Latin flavours from *merengue* to *son*. **ⓐ** C/ Aragó 141 **ⓣ** 934 514 564 **ⓦ** www.antillasalsa.com **ⓛ** 23.00–03.30 Mon–Wed & Sun, 23.00–04.00 Fri & Sat **ⓝ** Metro: Urgell

Buda Restaurante One of the Eixample's most glamorous nightspots with gilded furniture and chandeliers lighting the model cheekbones to perfection. Every night has a theme, from Geisha to Bollywood. **ⓐ** C/ Pau Claris 92 **ⓣ** 933 184 252 **ⓦ** www.budarestaurante.com **ⓛ** 21.00–03.00 **ⓝ** Metro: Catalunya

City Hall This small club's central location and summer terrace mean the dance floor is packed and throbbing to anything from deep house to electronica. **ⓐ** Rambla Catalunya 2–4 **ⓣ** 933 172 177 **ⓦ** www.grupo-ottozutz.com **ⓛ** 24.00–06.00 Tues–Sun **ⓝ** Metro: Catalunya

Distrito Diagonal See and be seen with the Eixample's beautiful people in this laid-back bar and nightclub. **ⓐ** Av. Diagonal 442 **ⓣ** 934 154 635 **ⓛ** 24.00–06.00 Fri & Sat **ⓝ** Metro: Diagonal. Admission charge (free before 04.00)

Xampanyería Casablanca A champagne bar fashioned after the Bogart-Bergman film, serving four kinds of house *cava* and tasty tapas. **ⓐ** C/ Bonavista 6 **ⓣ** 932 376 399 **ⓛ** 18.30–02.30 Thur–Sun, 18.30–03.00 Fri & Sat **ⓝ** Metro: Passeig de Gràcia

THEATRE, MUSIC & DANCE
Centre Artesà Tradicionàrius (CAT) Founded in 1993, the Tradicionàrius is devoted to the study, teaching and performance of Catalan traditional music and dance. **ⓐ** Travessera de Sant Antoni 6–8 **ⓣ** 932 184 485 **ⓦ** www.tradicionarius.com **ⓝ** Metro: Fontana

Montjuïc & El Raval

South of the city, the vast hill of Montjuïc is named 'Mountain of the Jews' after an early Jewish necropolis here. In 1929 it was the venue for the International Expo, and in 1992 it was the main site of the Barcelona Olympics. Today, with its top-notch sports facilities, together with some of the city's finest museums and galleries, it is a popular place for both locals and visitors at weekends. On the lower slopes of Montjuïc, the up-and-coming residential *barri* (quarter) of Poble Sec was once so poor it didn't even have a water supply, hence its name – 'Dry Village'. It joins the lively district of El Raval, also known as Barri Xinès (China Town), formerly a run-down area renowned as a centre of drugs, crime and prostitution. Nowadays, the upper part of the Raval has tidied up its act and, thanks to the opening of such institutions as the Museum of Contemporary Art (MACBA) and the neighbouring Contemporary Cultural Centre (CCCB), it is becoming newly fashionable, filled with galleries, fashion boutiques and chic cafés.

SIGHTS & ATTRACTIONS

L'Anella Olímpica (The Olympic Ring)

Santiago Calatrava's space-age communications tower dominates the skyline on Montjuïc hill. It marks the Olympic Ring – a monumental sports complex of concrete and marble, which served, in 1992, as the main venue for the Olympic Games. The Estadi Olímpic (Olympic Stadium) was originally designed in 1936 as an alternative venue to the Nazis' infamous Berlin Games. Today, highlights of the 1992 Games can be relived though memorabilia and video clips in the new Olympics museum situated beneath the stadium, which also has sporting artefacts such as Miguel Induraín's bicycle and virtual

enactments of performances, such as Bob Beamon's winning long jump. Also open to the public are the Picornell outdoor swimming pool and the state-of-the-art domed Palau Sant Jordi, which looks more like a UFO than an indoor sports arena. ❸ Av. de l'Estadi/ Passeig Olímpic, Montjuïc ❶ 934 260 660 (Galería Olímpica) ❾ www.fundaciobarcelonaolimpica.es ❶ 10.00–14.00, 16.00–19.00 Mon–Fri, Apr–Sept; 10.00–13.00, 16.00–18.00 Mon–Fri, Oct–Mar (Galería Olímpica) ❻ Bus: 50

Castell de Montjuïc (Montjuïc Castle)

This imposing 17th-century fortress, standing on the bluff of Montjuïc hill, has a dark history as prison and place of execution and torture in the Civil War, and was even used to bombard restless citizens into submission by Isabel II in 1842. Inside, the **Museu Militar** (Military Museum) contains an impressive collection of weaponry, maps, lead soldiers and uniforms. The bird's-eye views from the battlements are breathtaking. ❸ Ctra de Montjuïc 66 ❶ 933 298 613/ 933 298 613 ❶ 09.30–17.00 Tues–Fri, 09.30–20.00 Sat & Sun, Nov–Mar; 09.30–20.00 Tues–Sun, mid-Mar–Oct (museum) ❻ Metro: Paral.lel then funicular Teleféric; bus: 50

Palau Güell (Güell Palace)

This eccentric building, constructed in the 1880s and reopened in summer 2007 after extensive renovation, was Antoni Gaudí's first major architectural project. It was commissioned by the affluent industrialist Eusebi Güell, who shocked society by announcing he wished to move into C/ Nou de la Rambla, on the fringe of El Raval's notorious red-light district, rather than the fashionable new Eixample

◀ *The striking Torre de Calatrava at l'Anella Olímpica*

district, in order to be near his parents' home on La Rambla. Given the seedy neighbourhood, Gaudí created an austere façade resembling a fortress, with battlements, grilles like portcullises and wrought-iron dragons to fend off unwanted visitors.

The interior is lavishly decorated and fascinating. Follow the one-hour guided tour down to the cavernous basement stables, through various rooms decorated with *Modernista* furniture and fittings of wrought-iron, glass, ceramics and wood, and up to the rooftop terrace – an extraordinary forest of quirky finials and chimneys, decorated with coloured *trencadís* mosaics (broken ceramic pieces) and glass. The Güell family did not live here long as the palace was confiscated by Spanish Civil War anarchists in 1936, who used it as their military headquarters and prison. Today, it is protected as a UNESCO World Heritage Site. ❷ C/ Nou de la Rambla ❶ 933 173 974 ❺ 10.00–18.00 Mon–Sat (guided tours only)

Pavelló Mies van der Rohe (Mies van der Rohe Pavilion)

This masterpiece of modern rationalist design was created on the lower slopes of Montjuic hill as the German Pavilion for the 1929 International Expo by the celebrated Bauhaus architect Ludwig Mies van der Rohe. It was dismantled at the end of the fair and subsequently reconstructed in the 1980s to commemorate the centenary of his birth. It is a construction of astonishing simplicity, combining marble, onyx, glass, chrome and water using simple geometrical forms and clean lines. Its ultra-minimalist functional interior contains an exhibition on the architect's life and work, and includes his famous square-shaped leather and steel 'Barcelona Chair', created especially for the exhibition, which has since become an icon of modern design. ❷ Av. del Marquès de Comillas, Montjuïc ❶ 934 234 016 ❻ www.miesbcn.com ❺ 10.00–20.00 ❼ Metro: Espanya; bus: 13, 50, 100

Plaça d'Espanya

This bustling square and major traffic intersection was originally designed as a grand entrance to the 1929 Universal Exposition. The square itself is dominated by a classical-style monument designed by Gaudí's right-hand man, Josep Maria Jujol, and representing the three great rivers of Spain. The unusual Moorish-style building on one corner is the former bullring of Les Arenes, now converted into an ultra-modern leisure centre designed by Richard Rogers and known as the 'piazza in the sky'. It backs onto the recently renovated **Parc Joan Miró** (Joan Miró Park), with its startling 22 m (72 ft) high mosaic sculpture entitled *Dona i Ocell* (Woman and Bird).

Back in Plaça d'Espanya, a series of staircases, fountains and outdoor escalators leads you towards the impressive Palau Nacional and MNAC (see page 114). But the real crowd-puller is **La Font Màgica** (The Magic Fountain), which puts on illuminated musical fountain displays. ⓐ Pl. Espanya ⓛ Fountain displays 20.00–23.30 Thur–Sun; music every 30 mins 21.30–24.00 May–Sept, 19.00–21.00 Fri & Sat, Oct–Apr ⓝ Metro: Espanya

CULTURE

CaixaForum

The cultural nerve centre of Catalonia's biggest savings bank, La Caixa, lays on some of the best temporary art exhibitions in the whole city, ranging from photography to fine art, monographs to sculpture. No expense has been spared with the building either: the site was originally an enormous red brick textile factory built in grand industrial *Modernista* style by Josep Puig i Cadafalch in 1911; having fallen into dereliction by the end of the last century, La Caixa paid for its complete renovation, adding a white marble entrance plaza by Arata Isozaki,

a striking Sol LeWitt mural, a 350-seater auditorium for cultural performances and a library. ⓐ Casaramona, Av. Marquès de Comillas 6–8 ⓣ 934 768 600 ⓦ www.fundacio.lacaixa.es ⓛ 10.00–20.00 Tues–Sun ⓝ Metro: Espanya

Fundació Joan Miró (Joan Miró Foundation)

Fundació Joan Miró, on Montjuïc hill, pays homage to one of Barcelona's greatest artists. Famous for his childlike style and use of vivid primary colours, his work captures the very essence of this vibrant Mediterranean city. Miró was born in Barcelona in 1893 and spent much of his life here, developing his bold style and use of bright vibrant colours. The gallery, itself a work of art designed by Josep Lluís Sert, is a beautiful modern building of airy white spaces, massive windows and skylights set in gardens overlooking the city – and a perfect backdrop for 240 paintings, 175 sculptures, around 8,000 drawings, nine tapestries, four ceramics and his complete graphic works – the most complete collection of Miró's work in the world, many of which were donated to the Foundation by Miró himself.

The Foundation also stages temporary exhibitions of modern art, contemporary music recitals and a special permanent exhibition entitled 'To Joan Miró', including works by Calder, Ernst, Tàpies, Moore, Matisse and others, given to the Foundation in memory of the great Catalan surrealist. ⓐ Av. de Miramar, Montjuïc ⓣ 934 439 470 ⓦ www.bcn.fjmiro.es ⓛ 10.00–19.00 Tues–Sat (until 21.00 Thur), 10.00–14.30 Sun, closed Mon, Oct–June; 10.00–20.00 Tues–Sat (until 21.30 Thur), 10.00–14.30 Sun, closed Mon, July–Sept ⓝ Bus: 50, 55

◀ *Sculpture – and a great view – at the Fundació Joan Miró*

Museu d'Art Contemporani de Barcelona – MACBA
(Museum of Contemporary Art)

Hidden among the shabby narrow back streets in El Raval, this dazzling white glass-fronted museum comes as a something of a surprise, towering over the stark concrete Plaça dels Àngels. The dramatic building, with its swooping ramps, white-on-white décor and glass-walled galleries designed by American architect Richard Meier, was initially the subject of much controversy and almost upstages the art installations it contains. Nonetheless, it is regarded as one of the city's must-see galleries, focusing on the art movements of the second half of the 20th century, with special emphasis on Catalan and Spanish artists. Its extensive collection is exhibited in rotation, with works by Klee, Tàpies, Miró, Calder and Hurst among others. It also hosts temporary contemporary art exhibitions.
Ⓐ Pl. dels Àngels 1 ☎ 934 120 810 Ⓦ www.macba.es Ⓛ 11.00–19.30 Mon, Wed–Fri, 10.00–20.00 Sat, 10.00–15.00 Sun, closed Tues Ⓝ Metro: Catalunya. Admission charge

Museu Marítim (Maritime Museum)

The Maritime Museum is housed in the magnificent **Drassanes Reials** (Royal Shipyards), the largest and most complete medieval dockyards in the world. These impressive boatyards were built in the 13th century, at the height of Catalonia's maritime power, and are a triumph of Gothic civic architecture. Maps, charts, compasses, paintings, model ships, figureheads and countless other treasures of Barcelona's lengthy seafaring past fill their vast, church-like, stone-vaulted halls, and there are polyglot audio-guides to steer visitors around the key attractions.

Numerous boats are also on show, from the gold-medal-winning Flying Dutchman sloop raced by the Spanish sailing team at the Barcelona Olympics to a 60 m (197 ft) replica of the royal galley

La Real, flagship of Don Juan of Austria, which forms part of an exciting 45-minute multimedia spectacle 'The Great Sea Adventure'. The museum's flagship, the early 20th-century three-masted schooner *Santa Eulàlia* (renamed in honour of Barcelona's patron saint), is moored at the wooden pier at Barcelona's old port and is now also open to the public. ⓐ Av. de les Drassanes ⓣ 933 429 920 ⓦ www.museumaritimbarcelona.com ⓛ Museum: 10.00–20.00. Schooner: 12.00–19.30 Tues–Fri, 10.00–19.00 Sat & Sun, May–Oct; 12.00–17.30 Tues–Fri, 10.00–17.00 Sat & Sun, Nov–Apr ⓜ Metro: Drassanes. Admission charge

⬥ *The dramatic MACBA (Museum of Contemporary Art) building*

Museu Nacional d'Art de Catalunya – MNAC
(National Art Museum of Catalonia)

The staggering collections of the MNAC span a thousand years of Catalan art, from the 10th to the 20th centuries. They are housed in an imposing neoclassical palace, the Palau Nacional. Originally built as the symbol of the 1929 World Exhibition, it has recently been renovated by architect Gae Aulenti (who converted the Gare d'Orsay into one of Paris's foremost museums).

Among the MNAC's numerous treasures is one of the finest collections of medieval art in the world, divided into Romanesque and Gothic. The idea for this collection originated in the early 20th century, when theft of national architectural treasures was rife in Catalonia. The Romanesque Galleries trace the evolution of Catalan Romanesque art through a remarkable series of 11th- and 12th-century murals carefully stripped from the apses of churches throughout the region, and each painstakingly reconstructed in situ as if they were still in their original venues. There is also an impressive display of stone sculptures, wood carvings, gold and silverwork, altar cloths, enamels and coins. In contrast to the simplicity of the Romanesque style, the colourful Gothic collection presents over 400 highly ornate retables and sculptures, including an extraordinary 15th-century Virgin in full flamenco dress.

The Renaissance and baroque art section includes part of the dazzling Thyssen-Bornemisza Collection, formerly housed in Pedralbes Monastery (see page 125), containing predominantly 13th- to 18th-century Italian and German paintings, including works by Fra Angélico, Titian, Rubens, Canaletto and Velázquez.

The modern art collection is considered the most important ensemble of Catalan art from the 19th and early 20th centuries. It starts with works by Marià Fortuny, the earliest of the *Modernistes* and the first Catalan artist to be widely known abroad, through the less adventurous *Noucentista* (Noucentisme) movement and Impressionism to the avant-garde. There is also a new room dedicated exclusively to Pablo Picasso. The sculptures here are especially notable. However, the highlight of the collection is its decorative arts, a magnificent array of jewellery, textiles, stained glass and ceramics by such leading exponents of the era as Cadafalch and Gaudí.

The museum also includes an interesting display of photography, from its origins to the present day, and an important collection of coins, medals and papers from the 6th century BC to the present day.
ⓐ Palau Nacional, Montjuïc ⓣ 936 220 376 ⓦ www.mnac.es
ⓛ 10.00–19.00 Tues–Sat, 10.00–14.30 Sun, closed Mon ⓝ Metro: Espanya. Admission charge

RETAIL THERAPY

Considering the number of tourist attractions, Montjuïc is surprisingly devoid of boutiques. However, several museum shops (including Caixaforum, the MNAC and the Fundació Miró) stock a high-quality selection of designer items, books, gifts and arty souvenirs inspired by their collections. In the upper Raval, Carrer Doctor Dou and the surrounding streets have become a new centre of chic, filled with art galleries and fashion boutiques.

Poble Espanyol (Spanish Village)
This purpose-built 'Spanish Village' was originally conceived as a whistle-stop tour of the nation for the 1929 Universal Exposition. The life-sized village contains 117 reproductions of famous or characteristic buildings from all over Spain, many of which now

serve as art galleries and artisan workshops selling quality jewellery, wood carvings, leather items, and glass and ceramics, along with more tourist-oriented souvenirs. ⓐ Av. del Marquès de Comillas 13, Montjuïc ⓣ 933 257 866 ⓦ www.poble-espanyol.com ⓛ 09.00–20.00 Mon, 09.00–02.00 Tues–Thur, 09.00–04.00 Fri–Sat, 09.00–24.00 Sun, Mar–Dec; 09.00–20.00 Mon–Thur, 09.00–04.00 Fri–Sat, 09.00–24.00 Sun, Jan–Feb ⓜ Metro: Espanya; bus: 13, 50

TAKING A BREAK

Organic £ ❶ Probably the best vegetarian place in town, this refectory-style restaurant has friendly staff, a great all-you-can-eat salad bar, and all the veggie classics. ⓐ C/ Junta de Comerç 11 ⓣ 933 010 902 ⓛ 12.30–24.00 ⓜ Metro: Liceu

⬤ Figs and ametllat, *a traditional Catalan dessert made with almonds*

Soleá £ ❷ A sunny terrace bar on a quiet square with cheery orange décor and international snacks, from tacos to houmous and salad. ❸ Pl. del Sortidor 14 ❶ 934 410 124 ❺ 12.00–24.00 Tues–Sat, 12.00–16.00 Sun, closed Mon Ⓝ Metro: Poble Sec

Oleum ££ ❸ The new restaurant in the MNAC is a heavyweight on Barcelona's serious dining scene, with sweeping views, two Tàpies originals on the walls and an equally stunning menu of intricately presented delights. ❸ Palau Nacional ❶ 932 890 679 ❺ 13.00–16.00 Tues–Sun Ⓝ Metro: Espanya

AFTER DARK

RESTAURANTS

La Bella Napoli £ ❹ This jolly restaurant serves some of the best pizzas in town. ❸ C/ de Margarit 14 ❶ 934 425 056 ❺ 13.00–16.00, 20–23.00 Tues-Sun Ⓝ Metro: Paral.lel or Poble Sec

Quimet i Quimet £ ❺ Lined to the ceiling with a tremendous selection of wine, *cava* and spirits, this family-run joint serves some of the finest tapas in town, including preserved seafood and exquisite *montaditos* (snacks on little rounds of bread). ❸ C/ Poeta Cabanyes 25 ❶ 934 423 142 ❺ 12.00–16.00, 19.00–22.30 Mon–Fri, 12.00–16.00 Sat, closed Sun Ⓝ Metro: Paral.lel

Ca L'isidre £££ ❻ Despite its downmarket location in Poble Sec, this small bastion of contemporary Mediterranean cuisine counts King Juan Carlos among its regulars. ❸ C/ Les Flors 12 ❶ 934 411 139 Ⓦ www.calisidre.com ❺ 13.00–16.00, 20–23.00 Mon–Sat Ⓝ Metro: Paral.lel

Quo Vadis £££ ❼ Classic Spanish cuisine near the Liceu theatre (see page 65). There's even a special post-theatre menu. ⓐ C/ del Carme 7 ❶ 933 024 072 ⓦ www.restaurantquovadis.com ⓛ 13.00–16.00, 20–23.00 Mon-Sat Ⓜ Metro: Liceu

BARS, CLUBS & LIVE MUSIC

Estadi Olímpic The main venue for mega-star pop concerts, together with neighbouring Palau Sant Jordi. Tickets are best obtained through record shops. ⓐ Av. de l'Estadi ❶ 934 260 660 Ⓜ Bus: 13, 50

Jazz Sí Club The perfect bar for anyone serious about their jazz, with Cuban, rock and blues to boot. Each night is themed on a different genre: check the website for details. ⓐ C/ Requesens 2 ❶ 933 290 020 ⓦ www.tallerdemusics.com ⓛ 17.00–02.30 Mon–Thur & Sun, 17.00–03.00 Fri & Sat Ⓜ Metro: Sant Antoni

Pastis A tiny rustic bar with a bohemian atmosphere redolent of Paris's Latin Quarter. ⓐ C/ Santa Mònica 4 ❶ 933 187 980 ⓛ 19.30–02.30 Tues–Sun, closed Mon Ⓜ Metro: Drassanes

Sala Apolo This lively club, in an elegant old ballroom in the Poble Sec district, caters for all tastes and ages, with African, Latin and Spanish music, live bands and, at weekends, the popular DJ team Nitsa. ⓐ C/ Nou de la Rambla 113 ❶ 934 414 001 ⓦ www.sala-apolo.com ⓛ 24.00–05.00 Wed & Thur, 24.00–07.00 Fri & Sat Ⓜ Metro: Paral.lel

La Terrazza Dance till dawn under the stars to house and techno music at this summertime open-air club. ⓐ Poble Espanyol, Av. Marquès de Comillas s/n, Montjuïc ❶ 932 724 980 ⓛ 24.00–06.00 Thur–Sat, May–mid-Oct Ⓜ Metro: Espanya; bus: 13, 50

Tinta Roja With its dramatic bordello décor of red velvet and dusty chandeliers this atmospheric bar is the perfect place to enjoy a drink or an offbeat performance of flamenco or jazz on the tiny stage.
🅐 C/ Creu dels Molers 17 ☎ 934 433 243 🅦 www.tintaroja.net
🕑 20.00–02.00 Wed & Thur, 20.00–03.00 Fri & Sat
Ⓝ Metro: Poble Sec

ENTERTAINMENT

Centre de Cultura Contemporània de Barcelona (CCCB) This new arts centre, in a strikingly converted 19th-century workhouse, stages a wide variety of performance arts, including concerts, theatre, dance and film. 🅐 C/ del Montalegre 5 ☎ 933 064 100
🅦 www.cccb.org 🕑 11.00–20.00 Tues–Sat, 11.00–15.00 Sun, June–Sept; 11.00–14.00, 16.00–20.00 Tues & Thur–Fri, 11.00–20.00 Wed & Sat, 11.00–19.00 Sun, Sept–June Ⓝ Metro: Catalunya. Admission charge

Fundació Joan Miró The Miró Foundation (see page 111) contains Spain's chief centre for contemporary music development. It stages frequent concerts including the *Nits de Música* series in June and July. 🅐 Av. de Miramar, Parc de Montjuïc ☎ 934 439 470
🅦 www.bcn.fjmiro.es Ⓝ Bus: 50, 55

El Tablao de Carmen The flamenco shows here are touristic but fun. Advance booking is essential. 🅐 Poble Espanyol, Montjuïc
☎ 933 256 895 🅦 www.tablaodecarmen.com Ⓝ Bus: 13, 50

Pedralbes, Tibidabo & Les Corts

Pedralbes and Tibidabo are part of Barcelona's Zona Alta (Upper Zone), at a slightly higher elevation than the city centre. These smart hilly suburbs have been popular residential areas for centuries, with beautiful villas, gardens and parks draped over their hillsides. The area also contains some elegant restaurants and bars, but surprisingly few shops.

At 550 m (1,800 ft), Mont Tibidabo, part of the Collserola range, forms the north-western boundary of Barcelona. Pedralbes is situated at the top of the Avinguda Diagonal to the northwest of the city centre, and contains a beautiful medieval monastery and a Royal Palace with impressive ceramic and decorative arts collections. Immediately south of Pedralbes, the once rural *barri* of Les Corts (The Farmsheds) contains the stadium and museum of FC Barça, Barcelona's remarkable football team.

SIGHTS & ATTRACTIONS

Finca Güell

Every well-to-do member of the Barcelonan middle classes had a *finca* (country house) or a *torre* (villa) in the countryside at the turn of the 20th century and, as a consequence, the Zona Alta area is dotted with fine *Modernista* buildings. One such gem is Finca Güell, former holiday estate of the wealthy Güell family, ardent patrons of Antoni Gaudí. Today the building houses La Càtedra Gaudí, an institution specialising in subjects connected with this famous architect. Although the main buildings are closed to the public, it is still possible to admire his elaborate Moorish-style gatehouses and extraordinary gates depicting a dragon, a veritable masterpiece of *Modernisme* wrought-ironwork.

ⓐ Av. de Pedralbes 7 ❶ 932 045 250 🕘 09.00–13.00 Ⓝ Metro: Palau Reial

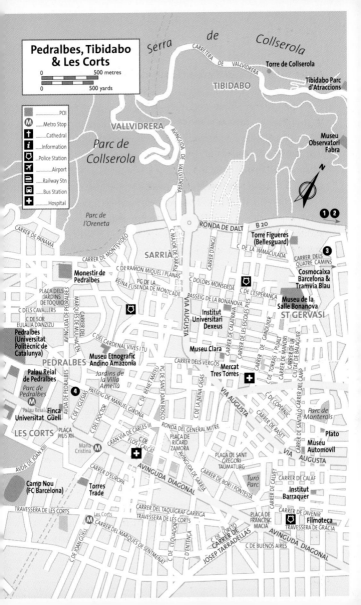

Museu del Futbol Club Barcelona (Museum of FC Barcelona)

If you can't get a ticket for a match, at least visit this – one of the city's most popular museums – and stand on the terraces of the second largest football stadium in the world (after Rio's Maracanã), with seating capacity for 120,000 fans. Barcelona is football-crazy and FC Barça is one of Catalonia's flagship institutions. Not only is it the fifth most successful business in Spain, but it is also the richest sports club in the world, with the largest membership of any soccer club.

The museum is under the terraces at Entrance 9, and contains a dazzling display of trophies, strips, photographic archives, audiovisual shows of famous match highlights and an impressive range of memorabilia documenting the history of football from its origins until the present day and, in particular, this club's extraordinary history as a political vehicle and as a rallying point for Catalans. ❸ Camp Nou – Estadi FCB (accesos 9), Av. Arístides Maillol ❶ 934 963 600 Ⓦ www.fcbarcelona.com ❻ 10.00–18.30 (stadium until 17.30) Mon–Sat, 10.00–14.30 (stadium until 13.30) Sun; 10.00–13.00 on match days (no stadium visits) Ⓜ Metro: Collblanc. Admission charge

Serra de Collserola (Collserola Range)

The hills of the Collserola range lie to the north and west of the city, forming a wonderful 6,550 ha (16,185 acres) nature reserve with extensive woodlands full of wildlife and meadows ablaze with wild flowers. Walking here is easy, as the paths and climbs are well maintained, with clearly defined picnic areas. This area is best accessed by taking an FGC train to Baixador de Vallvidrera, from where it is a short walk to the **information centre**, where details of walks and cycle routes are available. Nearby, British architect Norman Foster's glass-and-steel 268 m (879 ft) communications tower, the **Torre de Collserola** (Collserola Tower), whisks those with a head for heights up to an observation platform by glass-fronted lift for the most sensational views over the city and, on exceptionally clear days, as far as Mallorca. ❸ Centre d'Informacio, Parc de Collserola ❶ 932 803 552 ❷ 09.30–15.00 ❻ FGC Baixador de Vallvidrera

Tibidabo

Tibidabo is the highest peak of the Collserola range and the biggest draw for Barcelonans, who come especially at weekends to enjoy the superb views and the **Parc d'Atraccions**, an old-fashioned fairground of carousels, bumper cars, a hall of mirrors and a Ferris wheel, combined with a clutch of brand new high-tech attractions. Getting there, on an ancient tram and then by funicular, is all part of a fun family day out. No wonder locals nickname it La Muntanya Màgica (The Magic Mountain). Here too, the **Museu d'Autòmats del Tibidabo** contains a splendid collection of coin-operated fairground machines dating from the early 20th century. The modern **Sagrat Cor** (Sacred Heart) crowns the summit of Tibidabo – a neo-Gothic fantasy topped by a massive statue of Christ, visible for miles around. ❸ Parc d'Atraccions, Pl. del Tibidabo 3–4 ❶ 932 117 942 ❿ www.tibidabo.es ❷ 10.00–19.00/20.00, late Mar–early Oct; 12.00–22.00/23.00, July–Aug; 12.00–18.00 Sat & Sun only (winter) ❻ FGC: Av. del Tibidabo, plus Tramvia Blau and Funicular

WHAT'S IN A NAME?

The name 'Tibidabo' comes from the words uttered by Satan during his temptation of Christ in the wilderness: '*Haec omnia* **tibi dabo** (all these things will I give to you), *si cadens adoraberis me* (if thou wilt fall down and worship me)'.

Tramvía Blau (Blue Tram)

The electric Tramvía Blau is one of the last vestiges of the city's old tram system, in operation since 1902, and a true symbol of Barcelona's identity. Every 20 minutes it rattles along Avinguda Tibidabo between Plaça Kennedy and Plaça Doctor Andreu, passing many fine *Modernista* houses en route. At the end of the journey, take a table on the terrace of La Venta (see page 127). Then, take the **Funicular de Tibidabo** from here to the Parc d'Atraccions (see page 123) at Tibidabo's peak. 🕒 10.00–20.00 June–Sept; 10.00–18.00 Sept–June

CULTURE

Cosmocaixa Barcelona

The city's state-of-the-art science museum is located at the foot of Mont Collserola. It is divided into a number of sections including: the Geological Wall (illustrating Iberian geology); Archimedes

⬤ Take a trip on the electric Tramvía Blau

Gardens (an open-air space full of hands-on scientific experiments); a Planetarium; a Bubble Planetarium ; and the Flooded Forest (the first living Amazonian rainforest on display inside a science museum). This fascinating new centre is a must for budding scientists: the Toca Toca petting space allows children to encounter animals face to face; Clik (ages three to six) and Flash (ages seven to nine) are areas devoted to scientific experimentation for children. ❸ C/ Teodor Roviralta 47–51 ❶ 932 126 050 Ⓦ www.cosmocaixa.com ❸ 10.00–20.00 Tues–Sun, closed Mon Ⓝ FGC: Av. Tibidabo and then Tramvía Blau. Admission charge

Monestir de Pedralbes (Pedralbes Monastery)

This exquisite monastery was founded in 1326 by the Catalan King Jaume II and Queen Elisenda de Montcada for the nuns of the St Clare of Assisi order. The King died in 1327, just two years after their marriage, and Queen Elisenda spent the remaining 37 years of her life here. The Montcadas were among the most powerful families of their day and, under her auspices, the monastery grew rich and flourished. Today the monastery is still used by a small community of Clarista nuns.

The monastery takes its name from the Latin *petrae albae* (white stones), and is best seen in the elegant three-storey cloisters, which count among the city's finest medieval treasures. Enjoy the tranquillity of the central courtyard, fragrant with flowers and medicinal herbs, before visiting the refectory, chapter house, the Queen's grave and a series of beautifully painted prayer cells. Don't miss the Capella de Sant Miquel (St Michael's Cell), with its impressive 14th-century frescoes depicting the life of the Virgin and the Passion. ❸ Baixada del Monastir 9 ❶ 932 039 282 ❸ 10.00–14.00 Tues–Sun

Palau Reial de Pedralbes (Royal Palace of Pedralbes)

In 1919 the handsome villa of Can Feliu was converted into a royal residence for the King of Spain for the 1929 International Exhibition. After 1939, it was Franco's city residence and, following a handful of subsequent visits by royalty and heads of state, it was opened to the public in 1960. The impressive state rooms contain two museums. The **Museu de les Arts Decoratives** (Decorative Arts Museum ⓦ www.museuartsdecoratives.bcn.es) has an eclectic display of artefacts spanning the early Middle Ages to the present day, with special emphasis on the 20th century, most notably Modernism, Functionalism and Minimalism. The **Museu de la Ceràmica** (Ceramics Museum ⓦ museuceramica.bcn.es) traces Spanish ceramics from the 12th century, arranged by regional styles. Look out especially for the beautiful Catalan baroque panels *La Xocolatada* (The Chocolate Party) showing chocolate drinking at a garden party, and the atmospheric *La Cursa de Braus* (The Bullfight), as well as the impressive pieces by Miró and Picasso. The landscaped grounds make a lovely picnic venue, and there is even a fountain by Gaudí. ❸ Av. Diagonal 686 ❶ 932 801 621 🕙 10.00–14.00 Tues–Sun ⓝ Metro: Palau Reial; FGC: Reina Elisenda

RETAIL THERAPY

There are very few shops in this part of town. However, these two shopping centres should cater for most needs:

El Corte Inglés A branch of the city's foremost department store, selling everything from designer fashions to electronics, books, toys, jewellery and cosmetics. There is also a full supermarket, cafeteria and restaurant. ❸ Av. Diagonal 617 ❶ 933 667 100 ⓦ www.elcorteingles.es ⓝ Metro: Maria Christina

Pedralbes Centre This shopping centre, next door to El Corte Inglés, contains a wide variety of fashion, shoe, jewellery and design boutiques, including such names as Mango, Timberland and Armani Casa. There are also a handful of eateries and, during winter months, the square outside is turned into an ice rink.
🅐 Av. Diagonal 609–15 🕿 934 106 821 🌐 www.pedralbescentre.com
Ⓜ Metro: Maria Christina

TAKING A BREAK

La Venta £–££ ❶ This delightful Moorish-style open-air café at the foot of the Tibidabo funicular, with its glass conservatory and outdoor terrace, is the ideal venue for lunch or some light refreshment.
🅐 Pl. Doctor Andreu 🕿 932 126 455 🕒 13.30–15.15, 21.00–23.15 Mon–Sat, closed Sun Ⓜ FGC: Av. Tibidabo then Tramvia Blau

Merbeyé ££ ❷ An attractive cocktail bar tricked out in red velvet with a sleek terrace in the summer. 🅐 Pl. Doctor Andreu, Tibidabo 🕿 934 179 279 🕒 12.00–14.30 Mon–Thur, 12.00–03.30 Fri & Sat, 12.00–02.00 Sun Ⓜ FGC: Av. Tibidabo then Tramvia Blau or Bus 60

AFTER DARK

RESTAURANTS
La Balsa ££ ❸ Enjoy top-notch Catalan, Basque and Mediterranean cuisine accompanied by bird's-eye views of the city, served atop a circular tower originally built as a water cistern, near the science museum. 🅐 C/ Infanta Isabel 4 🕿 932 115 048 🕒 21.00–23.30 Mon, 14.00–15.30, 21.00–23.30 Tues–Sat, closed Sun, evening buffet only in August Ⓜ FGC: Av. del Tibidabo

Neichel £££ ❹ Located at the heart of Pedralbes, this is one of the city's finest restaurants, thanks to Alsace-born chef Jean-Louis Neichel, who boasts the accolade 'the most brilliant ambassador French cuisine has ever had within Spain'. ⓐ C/ Beltran y Rózpide 1–5 ⓣ 932 038 408 ⓦ www.neichel.es ⓛ Closed Sat lunch & all day Sun ⓝ Palau Reial

BARS, CLUBS & LIVE MUSIC

Danzatoria This fine mansion on the slopes of Tibidabo offers Barcelona's beautiful people four floors with different types of music (house, lounge, pop and chill out), rambling gardens and a huge terrace. ⓐ Av. Tibidabo 61 ⓣ 211 62 61 ⓦ www.danzatoria-barcelona.com ⓛ 19.00–03.00 Tue–Sun ⓝ FGC: Av. Tibidabo

Mirablau The chic set enjoy this stylish bar and garden terrace on Mont Tibidabo, with its spectacular views over the city and the port. It is especially romantic at dusk when the city lights start to twinkle. ⓐ Pl. Doctor Andreu 1 ⓣ 934 185 879 ⓛ 11.00–04.30 Mon–Thur, 11.00–05.30 Fri–Sun ⓝ FGC: Av. Tibidabo then Tramvía Blau

Tres Torres This sophisticated *Modernista* mansion with beautiful gardens, terrace, cocktail lounge and discotheque attracts a classy clientele to its elegant surroundings. On some nights there is live jazz or blues. ⓐ Via Augusta 300 ⓣ 932 051 608 ⓛ 17.00–03.00 ⓝ FGC: Tres Torres

▶ *Rolling Catalan countryside, Alt Penedès*

Tarragona & the Costa Daurada

It would be a shame to visit Barcelona without seeing some of the sights of Catalonia, with its beautiful landscapes and wide range of attractions, from wine tasting to rollercoaster rides. To the west, the Monestir de Montserrat is one of the most visited sights in Catalonia. South of Barcelona, the **Costa Daurada** (Golden Coast) is flanked by wide sandy beaches. Along with the popular wine-producing towns of Vilafranca del Penedès and Sant Sadurni d'Anoia, the two main destinations to visit here are Sitges, a delightful resort town that has a huge gay following, and the beautiful city of Tarragona, whose archaeological complex of ancient Roman treasures are a UNESCO World Heritage Site.

GETTING THERE

To get to Sitges, 40 miles (25 km) southwest of Barcelona, take the Renfe train from Passeig de Gracia, which takes about 45 minutes and leaves you in the centre of town. By car from the city or airport, take the southbound C32 following directions for Castelldelfels-Sitges. A taxi from the airport costs around 50 euros. The Renfe train to Tarragona takes about an hour from Passeig de Gracia and leaves you two minutes' walk from the foot of the Rambla Nova. By car, drive the A7 motorway southbound, exit number 33 (Tarragona/Valls), which will take you on to the N-240 and then on to Tarragona. For Vilafranca del Penedes, jump on the C4 Renfe Cercanias line from Plaça de Catalunya, which takes 55 minutes. By car, take the A2 motorway southbound.

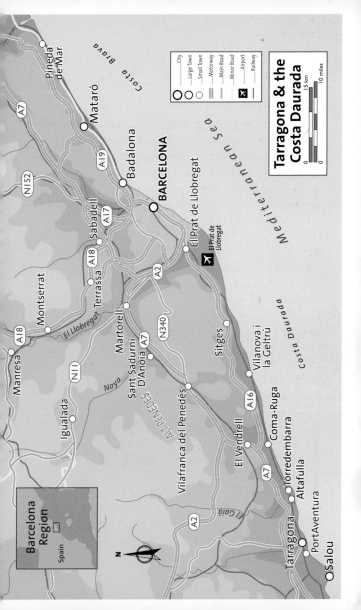

Tarragona & the Costa Daurada

- ⬤ City
- ◖ Large Town
- ◯ Small Town
- ▮▮ Motorway
- ▭ Main Road
- Minor Road
- ✈ Airport
- Railway

| 0 | 15 km |
| 0 | 10 miles |

Barcelona Region

Spain

Mediterranean Sea

Costa Brava

Costa Daurada

Pineda de Mar
Mataró
Badalona
BARCELONA
El Prat de Llobregat
El Prat de Llobregat ✈
Sitges
Vilanova i la Geltrú
Coma-Ruga
Torredembarra
Altafulla
Tarragona
PortAventura
Salou
El Vendrell
Vilafranca del Penedès
Sant Sadurni D'Anoia
Martorell
Terrassa
Sabadell
Montserrat
Manresa
Igualada

El Llobregat
Noya
ALT PENEDÈS
El Gaià

A7
A19
A17
A18
A18
N152
NII
N340
A2
A2
A7
A16
A7

N

SIGHTS & ATTRACTIONS

Alt Penedès

Just half an hour's southwest drive from Barcelona, the Alt Penedès is one of Spain's foremost wine-producing areas. Its two main towns, Sant Sadurni d'Anoia and Vilafranca del Penedès, have been producing wine since ancient times.

Vilafranca del Penedès is especially attractive, with beautiful arcaded streets, medieval mansions and an atmospheric Gothic quarter. Here too is the **Museu del Vi** (Wine Museum), showing the history and techniques of wine-making in Catalonia. The three main wineries (Mas Tinell, Romagosa Torné and Miguel Torres) are all located on the outskirts (in the direction of Sant Marti Sarroca), and offer tours and wine tastings (phone for details).

Nearby, Sant Sadurní d'Anoia is the centre of Catalonia's *cava* industry – producing 90 per cent of Spain's cava – with numerous producers dotted throughout the town. The largest, Codorníu, produces over 40 million bottles a year and its impressive *Modernista* plant is open to visitors for tours and tastings. Directly opposite the train station, Freixenet is another giant cava producer, also with tours and tastings. **Codorníu** ❶ 938 913 342 Ⓦ www.codorniu.es

THE LOCAL TIPPLE

The Alt Penedès region produces excellent red (*negre*), white (*blanc*) and rosé (*rosat*) wines as well as *cava*. Look out for *xampanyerías* (champagne bars) serving house cava by the glass, labelled according to quality and sweetness – *brut nature*, *brut*, *sec* and *semi-sec* (the sweetest and cheapest).

Freixenet ☎ 938 917 000 ⓦ www.freixenet.es
Mas Tinell ☎ 938 170 586 ⓦ www.mastinell.com
Miguel Torres ☎ 938 177 400 ⓦ www.torres.es
Museu del Vi ⓐ Pl. Jaume I 1–3, Vilafranca del Penedès ☎ 938 900 582
Romagosa Torné ☎ 938 991 353 ⓦ www.romagosatorne.com
Sant Sadurni d'Anoia Tourist Office ⓐ C/ Hospital 26 ☎ 938 913 188
ⓦ www.santsadurni.org
Vilafranca del Penedès Tourist Office ⓐ C/ Cort 14 ☎ 938 920 358
ⓦ www.vilafranca.org

Beaches

The Costa Daurada takes its name 'Golden Coast' from its broad
sandy beaches and is within easy reach of Barcelona and Tarragona.
Its resorts, including Salou, Altafulla, Torredembarra, Coma-Ruga and
Vilanova i la Geltrú, have a traditional seaside atmosphere and are
hugely popular with families. ⓦ www.costadaurada.org

Montserrat

Montserrat is located 56 km (35 miles) north-west of Barcelona, at the
summit of Catalonia's 1,200 m (4,000 ft) holy mountain (named after
its strangely serrated rock formations: *mont*, mountain; *serrat*, sawtooth).
Dramatically perched at the top of the mountain is Catalonia's most
revered pilgrimage site – the Monestir de Montserrat monastery. Every
year, thousands of worshippers take the thrilling cable-car ride up the
mountain to venerate a small medieval statue of the Madonna and
Child in the church, called *La Moreneta* (The Black Virgin), thought to
have been made by St Luke and brought here by St Peter and discovered
in a nearby cave in the 12th century. The statue has been blackened by
centuries of smoke from the millions of candles lit in her honour. The
monastery museum contains some important paintings by El Greco,

Picasso, Dalí and Caravaggio and every day at 13.00 one of Europe's oldest boys' choirs, La Escolania, sings in the church. Take the regular funicular service to the top of the mountains for wonderful walks, hikes and climbs around the various caves and hermitages. ☎ 938 777 701 🕐 08.00–10.30, 12.00–18.30 (church); 10.00–18.00 Mon–Fri, 09.30–18.30 Sat–Sun (museum) 🌐 www.abadiamontserrat.net

Sitges

Just 40 km (25 miles) south of Barcelona, the attractive beach resort of Sitges has long been a holiday playground of Barcelonans, celebrated for its beautiful Platja d'Or (Golden Beach) that stretches southwards for 5 km (3 miles) from the baroque church of Sant Bartomeu i Santa Tecla. The old town itself is full of bohemian charm, with its narrow streets of flower-bedecked whitewashed cottages, and attractive *Modernista* buildings. From the mid-19th century, Sitges attracted artists and writers, a movement kicked off by *Modernista* painter Santiago Rusinyol, whose villa – Cau Ferrat – is now a must-see museum. The palm-fringed promenade is lined with beach bars, cafés and fish restaurants. However, Sitges is perhaps best known today for its vibrant nightlife. It is also a popular gay holiday destination and comes alive for the outrageous carnival celebrations in February. **Tourist Office** ❸ C/ Sínia Morera 1 ☎ 938 945 004 🌐 www.sitgestur.com

Tarragona

Located on a rocky bluff just 97 km (60 miles) southwest of Barcelona, Tarragona boasts the largest ensemble of Roman remains in Spain – the extraordinary architectural legacy of Roman *Tarraco*, former capital of the Iberian peninsula. The Romans captured Tarragona in 218 BC and it became the home of Julius Caesar, and the base for the Roman conquest of Spain. It was also the main commercial centre on this stretch of coast until the 12th century, when Barcelona overshadowed it following the Christian reconquest of the nation.

The Roman remains in the city are remarkable. The **Amfiteatre Romà** (amphitheatre) is cut into the hillside overlooking the Mediterranean. This is where the Romans held their public spectacles, including gladiator fights, before an audience of 12,000 people. During the 12th century, the Romanesque church of Santa Maria del Miracle was built on the site. The **Museu d'Història** (Tarragona History Museum) traces the history of the city through an astonishing array of ancient treasures, while the equally fascinating **Museu Nacional Arqueològic** (Archaeological Museum) includes a section of the old Roman wall together with busts of emperors, sarcophagi and some beautiful mosaics. Walk the

🔽 *The Platja d'Or and church of Sant Bartomeu i Santa Tecla at Sitges*

Passeig Arqueològic, a promenade around the Roman walls for excellent views of the city and the hinterland of the Camp de Tarragona.

A short walk from the city centre, the **Museu i Necropolia Palaeocristians** (Palaeo-Christian Museum) contains the city's most treasured Roman remains in a former necropolis, with superb mosaics, glass, pottery and ivory.

With so many Roman treasures, it would be easy to overlook Tarragona's mighty Catedral – a magnificent Romanesque-Gothic construction in the form of a cross, created at the highest point of the city as the centrepiece of the *ciutat vella* (old city).

Amfiteatre Romà ⓐ Parc del Miracle ⓣ 977 242 220 ⓛ 09.00–21.00 Easter week–Sept; 09.00–17.00 Oct–Easter

Catedral ⓐ Pl. de la Seu ⓣ 977 238 685 ⓛ 10.00–13.00, 16.00–19.00 Mon–Sat, mid-Mar–May; 10.00–19.00 Mon–Sat, June–mid-Oct; 10.00–17.00 Mon–Sat, mid-Oct–mid-Nov; 10.00–14.00 Mon–Sat, mid-Nov–mid-Mar

Museu d'Història ⓐ Pl. del Rei ⓣ 977 236 209 ⓦ www.museutgn.com ⓛ 09.00–21.00 Tues–Sat, 09.00–15.00 Sun, June–Sept; 10.00–13.30, 15.30–18.30 Tues–Sat, 10.00–14.00 Sun, Oct–May

Museu Nacional Arqueològic ⓐ Pl. del Rei 5 ⓣ 977 236 209 ⓦ www.mnat.es

Museu i Necropolia Palaeocristians ⓐ Passeig de la Independència ⓣ 977 211 175

Passeig Arqueològic ⓐ El Portal del Roser ⓣ 977 245 796 ⓛ 09.00–21.00 Tues–Sat, 09.00–15.00 Sun, May–Sept; 09.00–19.00 Tues–Sun, Oct–Mar

Tarragona Tourist Office ⓐ C/ Major 39 ⓣ 977 250 795 ⓦ www.tarragonaturisme.es

Universal Mediterrànea Port Aventura

A short distance (67 miles/108 km) south of Barcelona near Tarragona, Port Aventura is one of Europe's biggest and best theme parks. Catalonia's answer to Disneyland is an entertaining day out for all the family, with its exotic shows and fairground rides in themed Mexican, Chinese, Polynesian, Wild West and Mediterranean settings. Don't miss the Dragon Khan, Europe's largest rollercoaster with a stomach-churning eight 360° loops or the Costa Caribe water park.

ⓐ Port Aventura, near Tarragona ⓣ 977 779 090 ⓛ 10.00–19.00 Mar–June, Sept–Oct; 10.00–24.00 July & Aug. Check website for other opening times ⓦ www.portaventura.es ⓝ Train from Passeig de Gràcia/by car, take the A2 and then the A7 or the N340. Admission charge

Villa Casals, Sant Salvador

The celebrated Barcelonan cellist, Pablo Casals (1876–1973), built a summer residence near the beach in the delightful town of Sant

⬥ *Tarragona – the atmospheric old city*

Salvador. Today it contains a museum in his honour, documenting the life and work of this musical genius. A veritable child prodigy, he started out on a homemade instrument constructed from a broom handle, a large gourd and some gut strings, and by the age of four he could play the violin, piano, flute and organ. His solo debut in Paris in 1899 launched a touring career that made him famous worldwide. Eventually, in 1920 he started conducting and founded his own orchestra in Barcelona until 1939, when he was forced into exile. He never returned to his house here, but one year after his death it was inaugurated as a museum. ❸ Av. Palfuriana 59, Sant Salvador ❶ 977 684 276 ⓦ www.paucasals.org ◷ 10.00–14.00, 16.00–18.00 Tues–Fri, 10.00–14.00, 16.00–19.00 Sat, 10.00–14.00 Sun, mid-Sept–mid-June; 10.00–14.00, 17.00–21.00 Tues–Sat, 10.00–14.00 Sun, mid-June–mid-Sept. Admission charge

RETAIL THERAPY

Shopping here doesn't match Barcelona for choice or style, but Tarragona has some reasonable shops and fashion boutiques, most notably along and around La Rambla Nova and in the Centro Comercial Parc Central on Avinguda Roma. Sitges has some quirky boutiques and fun gift shops, and be sure to stop at one of the many wineries in Vilafranca del Penedès or Sant Sadurní di Anoia to stock up your wine cellar.

TAKING A BREAK

Coma-Ruga
Casa Victor £ A popular tapas bar adjoining a smart seafood restaurant on the seafront. ❸ Passeig Marítim 23 ❶ 977 681 473

Vilafranca del Penedès

Inzolia £ A wine shop and excellent bar specialising, of course, in local wines from Vilafranca. ⓐ C/ Palma 21 ⓣ 938 181 938

AFTER DARK

RESTAURANTS

Montserrat

Abat Cisneros ££ Traditional Catalan specialities in former 16th-century monastery stables. ⓐ Hotel Abat Cisneros, Pl. de Monestir ⓣ 938 777 701

Sitges

Mare Nostrum ££ Sophisticated fish restaurant on the seafront. Try the special Xato de Sitges (grilled fish with romesco sauce). ⓐ Passeig de la Ribera 60–2 ⓣ 938 943 393

Tarragona

Estacio Marítima £££ Top-notch fish restaurant in the atmospheric fishermen's district of Serralló. ⓐ Moll de Costa Tinglado 4 ⓣ 977 232 759

Vilafranca del Penedès

Cal Ton ££ Modern minimalist restaurant serving inspiring Catalan cuisine with a twist. ⓐ C/ del Casal 8 ⓣ 938 903 741

NIGHTLIFE

Tarragona has plenty of outdoor cafés and bars in its beach resorts, some with live music. Sitges' most famous street is Carrer Primer de Maig, AKA Sin Street, packed with bars and the main route for carnival. Renowned for its gay scene, there are dozens of gay bars in Carrer Sant Bonaventura alone. Mediterráneo (ⓐ C/ Sant Bonaventura 6)

is the largest gay disco. Other popular venues include lesbian joint Mari Pili (ⓐ C/ Joan Tarrida Ferratges 14) and Trailer (C/ Angel Vidal 36), with its infamous foam parties.

ACCOMMODATION

HOTELS
Montserrat
Abat Cisneros £ A pleasant 3-star hotel with cheap, basic rooms in former monks' cells. ⓐ Pl. de Monestir ⓣ 938 350 201

Sitges
El Xalet £ This small tranquil hotel is housed in a beautiful *Modernista* villa with an outdoor pool and garden. ⓐ C/ Illa de Cuba 33–5 ⓣ 938 110 070 Ⓦ www.elxalet.com

Hotel Liberty £–££ Large, airy rooms overlooking a lushly planted garden in a perfectly central location. ⓐ C/ Illa de Cuba 45 ⓣ 938 110 872 Ⓦ www.libertyhotelsitges.com

Dolce Sitges £££ Stay with the beautiful people at this cutting-edge new 5-star hotel on the outskirts of town. ⓐ Av. Camí de Miralpeix 12 ⓣ 938 109 000 Ⓦ www.sitges.dolce.com

Tarragona
Husa Imperial Tarraco ££ The best hotel in town, with superb views of the coast and the Roman amphitheatre. ⓐ Passeig Palmeres ⓣ 977 233 040 Ⓦ www.husa.es

---

◗ *Barcelona's efficient metro network, operated by TMB*

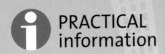

PRACTICAL information

Directory

GETTING THERE
By air

Barcelona's El Prat de Llobregat Airport (☎ 932 983 838 🆆 www.aena.es) is increasingly well served by low-cost airlines from various UK and European destinations. The airport has three terminals (A, B and C), and a new south terminal, which should be completed by early 2009, all linked by a walkway. Foreign airlines mostly use the newly expanded terminal A, while Iberia, the national airline, generally uses terminal B. Terminal C is used mainly for domestic flights. There are easy connections to the city by bus, train and taxi. As part of the major expansion, a new train station will be built nearby, connecting the airport to the Spanish high-speed AVE network, and to both Line 2 and Line 9 of the Barcelona Metro.

The flight time from London is approximately two hours. If you are struggling to find a cheap ticket, it is also worth considering flying with Ryanair, or a charter company such as First Choice Airways, into Girona-Costa Brava airport, which is only 112 km (70 miles) away – just one and a half hours by car or train to Barcelona. Ryanair also flies into Reus, some 100 km (65 miles) south of Barcelona. The best deals can be found by booking well in advance through the websites of leading airlines and tour operators.

Visitors from the USA can fly directly with Iberia, or take a connecting flight in Madrid or one of the other main European hubs.

British Airways ☎ (UK) 0870 850 9850, (Spain) 902 111 333
🆆 www.britishairways.com

easyJet ☎ (Barcelona) 933 792 720 🆆 www.easyjet.com

First Choice Airways ☎ (UK) 0870 850 3999 🆆 www.firstchoice.co.uk

Iberia ☎ (UK) 0870 609 0500, (Spain) 902 400 500 🆆 www.iberia.com

Ryanair ☎ (Girona and Reus) 972 473 650 🆆 www.ryanair.com

Many people are aware that air travel emits CO_2, which contributes to climate change. You may be interested in the possibility of lessening the environmental impact of your flight through Climate Care, which offsets your CO_2 by funding environmental projects around the world. Visit Ⓦ www.climatecare.org.

By road
The usual route from the UK by car involves driving down through France and across the Pyrenees to Barcelona. It is advisable to plan your route in advance with a detailed map and to allow at least two days for the journey. Remember to drive on the right, wear your seatbelt at all times and stick to the speed limits: 120 kph (74 mph) on motorways, 100 kph (62 mph) on dual carriageways, 90 kph (56 mph) on other roads, except in urban areas where it is 50 kph (31 mph) unless otherwise stated.

The journey from London to Barcelona by coach takes around 26 hours. Contact Eurolines for further information.
Eurolines ℹ (UK) 08705 143219, (Spain) 902 405 040 Ⓦ www.eurolines.es

By rail
RENFE, the Spanish rail network, links Barcelona to Madrid and other major cities in Spain and abroad. Seat reservations are required on all intercity trains. It takes just 15 hours by train from London via the Channel Tunnel to Barcelona. Contact Rail Europe for further information.
Rail Europe Ⓦ www.raileurope.com
RENFE ℹ 902 240 202 Ⓦ www.renfe.es

By water
The Port de Barcelona is the second largest cruise centre in the Mediterranean after Athens. There are a total of seven cruise ship

terminals (including four at Moll Adossat, Moll de Sant Bernat, Port Vell by the Maremàgnum shopping centre at the foot of the Ramblas and the North and South terminals), each with tourist information centres, bureaux de change, first-aid facilities, car hire, shops, bars and restaurants.

There are also regular ferries from the Balearic islands of Mallorca, Menorca and Ibiza, operated by Trasmediterránea, as well as a fast ferry service between Palma and Barcelona.

Autoritat Portuària de Barcelona Ⓦ www.apb.es

Trasmediterránea ⓣ 902 454 645 Ⓦ www.trasmediterranea.es

ENTRY FORMALITIES

Citizens of EU countries, USA, Canada, Australia, New Zealand, South Africa and Ireland who hold valid passports do not need a visa to visit Spain for less than 90 days. Other visitors should check with their nearest Spanish consulate.

Visitors to Barcelona from within the EU are entitled to bring their personal effects and goods for personal consumption and not for resale, up to a total of 800 cigarettes and 10 litres of spirits. Duty-free limits for those entering from outside the EU are 200 cigarettes (50 cigars, 250 g tobacco), 1 litre of spirits or 2 litres of wine. No meat or dairy produce is permitted into the country from inside or outside the EU.

MONEY

Spain's currency is the euro, with notes issued in denominations of 5, 10, 20, 50 and 100 euros, and coins of 1 and 2 euros and also 1, 2, 5, 10, 20 and 50 cents. Credit cards are widely used in Barcelona (especially VISA, MasterCard, AMEX and Diners Club) and most UK banks' cash cards can be used to obtain cash in local currency from some ATMs, although the commission charged can be expensive.

HEALTH, SAFETY & CRIME

The water in Barcelona is safe to drink although most people prefer to drink bottled water – either still (*aigua sense gas/agua sin gas*) or carbonated (*aigua amb gas/agua con gas*). A change of diet could lead to stomach upsets, so carry a supply of anti-diarrhoea tablets just in case.

Thanks to a reciprocal healthcare agreement, nationals of EU countries and some other countries can get reduced-price, sometimes free, medical treatment in Spain on presentation of a valid European Health Insurance Card (EHIC), the replacement for the E111 that ceased to be valid on 31 December 2005. This card gives access to state-provided medical treatment only. Apply on-line for an EHIC at www.dh.gov.uk/travellers and allow at least 2–3 weeks to receive the card. On top of this, private medical insurance is still advised and is essential for all other visitors. If you need to consult an English-speaking doctor, ask for help at your hotel reception or call the Centre Mèdic Assistencial de Catalunya (❸ C/ Provença 281 ❶ 932 153 793 ❺ 08.00–20.00 Mon–Fri); see also page 154 for emergency medical aid.

Violent crime is rare in Barcelona but the petty crime rate (pickpocketing, purse-snatching and so on) is high, especially in the Barri Gòtic around La Rambla, Plaça Reial and in El Raval. Don't carry excess cash, and use the hotel safe for valuable goods; don't leave anything visible in a parked car; beware of pickpockets in crowded places (especially on La Rambla); and stick to well-lit populated areas by night. The Guàrdia Urbana (in navy and pale blue uniforms) and increasingly the Mossos d'Esquadra (in navy and light blue uniforms with a red trim) keep law and order in the city and are generally helpful in minor cases of crime and security. If you need a police station, ask for *la comisaría*. (See also page 154 for emergency police assistance.)

TRAVEL INSURANCE
Whichever mode of transport you choose, make sure you have adequate personal travel insurance for the trip. The policy should give cover for medical expenses, loss, theft, repatriation, personal liability and cancellation expenses. If you are travelling in your own vehicle, you should also check that you are properly insured, and remember to take your driving licence and all relevant insurance documents with you.

OPENING HOURS

Banks: Most banks open 08.30–14.00 Mon–Fri. Some main branches also open 08.30–12.30 on Saturdays.

Businesses: Business hours are generally 08.00/09.00–18.00/19.00 Mon–Fri, with a siesta around 13.30–15.30/16.00.

Museums: Museum hours vary. Museums are generally closed on Sunday afternoon and all day Monday and some of the smaller museums close for the lunchtime siesta.

Shops: Large shops and chains open from 10.00 to 20.00/21.00 Monday to Saturday. Most smaller or independent shops open 09.00/10.00 until around 14.00, then again around 16.30–20.00/21.00 Monday to Saturday. On Sunday all shops are closed except for bakeries (morning only), kiosks and shops in licensed tourist zones such as the Maremàgnum shopping centre and La Rambla. Market times vary, but the city's food markets (including La Boqueria) are generally open every morning Mon–Sat.

TOILETS

With the exception of the most central beaches, it is difficult to find public toilets in the city, so you are best advised to rely on the facilities provided in museums, galleries, shops, bars and restaurants, which are usually free.

CHILDREN

Children receive a warm welcome in Barcelona, and they are welcomed rather than tolerated in cafés, restaurants and even bars even though very few restaurants offer specific children's menus. Nappies, baby food and formula milk can be bought from supermarkets and pharmacies but, if you have a preferred brand take a supply with you. If you need to hire a car seat for a child, double-check availability when making the booking and also check the seat carefully before fitting. Ask your hotel reception about babysitters and local crèches. Some hotels offer a baby-listening service for the evenings.

There are great parks and playgrounds for children to enjoy throughout the city, and lovely sandy beaches. Many of the museums and attractions also appeal to children and even some of the city's transportation modes are entertaining, especially the cable cars and funiculars. The following activities are guaranteed to keep the kids entertained:

- **L'Aquàrium** (see page 72) Special hands-on exhibits and a fascinating underwater tunnel.
- **Beaches** (see page 74) Beautiful sandy beaches with playgrounds, shops, showers and lifeguards. At Nova Mar Bella, there are small boats for hire in summer.
- **Camp Nou** (see page 122) One of the world's biggest football stadiums and home to FC Barça.
- **Cosmocaixa** (see page 124) The spectacular new science museum and planetarium appeals to all ages with special hands-on experiments in the Clik and Flash areas.

- **La Font Màgica** (see page 109) A spectacular sound-and-light extravaganza.
- **Port Aventura** (see page 134) One of Europe's largest theme parks, just south of Tarragona.
- **Las Golondrinas** (see page 77) Boat trips around the harbour and to the Olympic port.
- **IMAX** (see page 86) Larger than life movies.
- **MACBA** (see page 112) Older children find the modern art installations amusing.
- **Museu d'Història de Catalunya** (see page 80) This state-of-the-art educational museum is great fun for older children, with loads of interactive sections.
- **Museu Marítim** (see page 112) It's fun to climb aboard the boats and to experience life at sea.
- **Museu Xocolata** (see page 79) Chocolate models of famous Barcelona buildings and landmarks.
- **Parc d'Atraccions, Tibidabo** (see page 123) Old-fashioned fairground on top of Mont Tibidabo.
- **Parc de la Ciutadella** (see page 77) A boating-lake and a life-size elephant statue.
- **Parc Zoològic** (see page 77) The city zoo appeals to children young and old.
- **La Rambla** (see page 58) Small children find the street entertainments fascinating here.

LANGUAGE

Barcelona is a bilingual city with two official languages, Catalan and (Castilian) Spanish. Catalan is not a dialect but a distinct language with a long and proud history. It is spoken by over six million people and understood by 11 million (in Catalonia, Valencia, the Balearic islands, Roussillon in southern France, Andorra, and Alghero in Sardinia). Most Barcelonans are bilingual and switch back and forth between Catalan and Spanish depending on who they are talking to.

Most hotels, museum and tourist office staff will speak some English but any attempt to speak Spanish, rather than English, will go down well. However, if you can manage a few words of Catalan, you'll really win people over.

COMMUNICATIONS

Phones

Public phones take coins, phone cards and credit cards, and have instructions for use in English. Buy phone cards from post offices and tobacconists. Spain has an excellent mobile phone network.

The Spanish Yellow Pages (Páginas Amarillas, ⓦ www.paginasamarillas.es) is a useful source for telephone numbers.

International enquiries ⓣ 11825
National enquiries ⓣ 11818
Operator ⓣ 1002

Post

The Spanish postal service is moderately efficient and its bright yellow offices (*Correus/Correos*) and post boxes are easy to spot. The central office is at Plaça Antonio López, Barri Gòtic (ⓣ 934 868 050 ⓛ 08.30–21.00 Mon–Fri, 08.30am–14.00 Sat). Take a numbered ticket from the machines by the entrance and wait for your turn. Stamps can be purchased at post offices and tobacconists. It costs €0.58 to send a postcard to Europe and €0.78 to the rest of the world.

TELEPHONING SPAIN

To phone Spain from abroad, dial the international access code (00) followed by the country code 34. All telephone numbers in Barcelona begin with 93 followed by a seven-digit number.

TELEPHONING ABROAD

To phone home from Barcelona, dial the international access code (00) followed by the relevant country code: UK 44, USA and Canada 1, Australia 61, New Zealand 64, Republic of Ireland 353, South Africa 72, then the local code (minus the initial 0) and finally the number you want.

Internet cafés

Many hotels and hostels now offer internet access and there are cybercafés dotted all over the city including:

Bar Daguiri A bar by the beach with free internet access. Bring along your laptop and they will wire you up. ⓐ C/ Grau i Torras 59 ⓣ 932 215 109 Ⓜ Metro: Barceloneta

Bornet A popular internet café in front of the Picasso Museum. ⓐ Barra de Ferro 3 ⓣ 933 194 698

Electric Lounge An internet café-lounge by the cathedral, with free coffee. ⓐ C/ Misser Ferrer 1 ⓣ 933 041 616 Ⓦ www.electric-barcelona.com

ELECTRICITY

Electricity is supplied at 220–5 volts. Spanish plugs are of the two-pin round plug variety, so an adapter will be required for British and non-Continental appliances. US and other visitors with 110-volt appliances will need to use a voltage transformer too.

The Plaça d'Espanya is one of the city's major traffic intersections

TRAVELLERS WITH DISABILITIES

Most of the city's modern attractions (such as MACBA and Cosmocaixa), along with many buses and the newest metro line 2 (purple), have good access for those with disabilities. However, in the narrow streets and ancient buildings of the historic centre and in some of the *Modernista* houses, access is poor. All new buildings are now, by law, disabled-friendly. For taxis adapted to persons with reduced mobility, call ☎ 934 208 088. The tourist offices can provide further useful addresses.

For further information contact:

Disabled Persons Transport Advisory Committee (UK)
🌐 www.dptac.gov.uk/door-to-door

Society for Accessible Travel & Hospitality (STH) Advice for US-based travellers with disabilities. ☎ 212 447 7284 🌐 www.sath.org

Trip Scope Advice for UK-based travellers with disabilities.
🕿 08457 585641 Ⓦ www.tripscope.org.uk

TOURIST INFORMATION

Barcelona's Tourist Information Offices (*Turisme de Barcelona*) are useful for maps, accommodation, attractions and event information and any other queries you have about the city. There are several branches:

Airport Ⓐ Terminals A & B 🕒 09.00–21.00, closed 25 Dec and 1 Jan
Plaça de Catalunya Ⓐ Pl. de Catalunya 17–S (main office)
🕒 09.00–21.00, closed 1 Jan and 25 Dec
Plaça Sant Jaume Ⓐ C/ Ciutat 2 🕒 09.00–20.00 Mon–Fri, 10.00–20.00 Sat, 10.00–14.00 Sun and public holidays
Sants Railway Station Ⓐ Pl. Països Catalans 🕒 08.00–20.00 (summer); 08.00–20.00 Mon–Fri, 08.00–14.00 Sat & Sun and public holidays (winter), closed 25–6 Dec, 1 Jan

There are also a number of information booths at strategic points around the city:
Columbus Monument Ⓐ Pl. Portal de la Pau 🕒 09.00–21.00
Estació del Nord Ⓐ C/ Alí Bei 80 🕒 09.30–14.30 Mon–Sat
Plaça Espanya Ⓐ Av. Maria Cristina/Pl Espanya 🕒 10.00–20.00 July–Sept; 10.00–16.00 Oct–June
Sagrada Família Ⓐ C/ Sardenya (in front of the Passion façade)
🕒 10.00–20.00 July–Sept; 10.00–16.00 Oct–June

The tourist office also has a multilingual call centre for general tourist information 🕿 807 117 222 (from Spain); 932 853 834 (from abroad). Its official website, together with the Spanish National Tourist Office, provides further details (in English, French, Spanish and

Catalan) about the city and the region, its history, events and facilities.

Spanish National Tourist Office Ⓦ www.tourspain.es

Turisme de Barcelona Ⓦ www.barcelonaturisme.com

For further information on the city's acclaimed *Modernista* architecture and the *Ruta del Modernisme* (a self-guided walking route past many of the city Modernist highlights), contact the **Centre del Modernisme** ⓐ Casa Amatller, Passeig de Gràcia 41 ⓣ 934 880 139

BACKGROUND READING

An Olympic Death, Manuel Vázquez Montalbán – crime novel, written just before the 1992 Olympics, with a Barcelona native as the central detective character.

Barcelona Design Guide, Juliet Pomés Leiz & Ricardo Feriche – a comprehensive guide to Barcelona's 'designer' culture.

Barcelona: The Great Enchantress, Robert Hughes – a 21st-century portrait of the city.

Barcelonas, Manuel Vázquez Montalbán – reflections on the city by one of its most prominent modern authors.

The Best of Worlds, Quim Monzo – black humour with Barcelona as its backdrop, by Catalonia's best-selling author.

Homage to Barcelona, Colm Tóibín – a fascinating account of the city, its art and architecture.

Homage to Catalonia, George Orwell – first-hand observations of life in the region during the Spanish Civil War.

The Shadow of the Wind, Carlos Ruiz Zafón – this mystery story set in 1950s Barcelona was a runaway bestseller.

The Time of the Doves, Merce Rodoreda – novel set in the city during the Civil War, by one of Catalonia's most celebrated women writers.

Emergencies

EMERGENCY NUMBERS
Ambulance ❶ 061
Emergency (Catalonia) ❶ 112
Fire ❶ 080
Guardia Urbana (City police) ❶ 092
Mossos d'Esquadra (Emergencies and traffic accidents) ❶ 088
Policía Nacional (National police) ❶ 091

MEDICAL SERVICES
Should you become seriously ill, lists of local doctors (*medicos*),
dentists (*dentistas*) and hospitals can be found in telephone
directories or by contacting your consulate, who will have lists of
English-speaking practitioners. Alternatively, ask your hotel reception
to help or, in a real emergency, dial 061 for an ambulance. If you have
a valid European Health Insurance Card (EHIC, see page 145), you
should ensure that the doctor is part of the Spanish healthcare
system as the card covers only state-provided medical treatment.

Pharmacies (*farmàcies*) are widespread, and their highly trained
staff can provide medical advice and over-the-counter drugs. In an

EMERGENCY PHRASES

Help! ¡Socorro! *¡Sawkoro!*
Fire! ¡Fuego! *¡Fwegoh!*
Stop! ¡Stop! *¡Stop!*

emergency, go straight to the city centre casualty department, Centre d'Urgències Perecamps ⓐ Av. de les Drassanes 13–15 ⓣ 934 410 600 ⓝ Metro: Drassanes

THE POLICE
There are several police stations throughout the city including:
Barceloneta ⓐ Passeig Joan de Borbó 32 ⓣ 932 240 600
Eixample ⓐ C/ de Guadalajara 3 ⓣ 932 903 021
El Raval ⓐ C/ Nou de la Rambla 78–80 ⓣ 932 902 844

There is also a multilingual police service at the Guardia Urbana station on La Rambla near Plaça Reial.
Guardia Urbana de Ciutat Vella ⓐ La Rambla 43 ⓣ 932 562 430

EMBASSIES & CONSULATES
Australian ⓐ Pl. Gala Placidia 1, Barcelona ⓣ 934 309 013
British ⓐ Av. Diagonal 477, Barcelona ⓣ 933 666 200
Canadian ⓐ C/ Elisenda de Pinós 10, Barcelona ⓣ 932 042 700
Irish ⓐ Gran Via Carlos III, 94, Barcelona ⓣ 934 915 021
New Zealand ⓐ Travesera de Gràcia 64, Barcelona ⓣ 932 090 399
South African ⓐ C/ Claudio Coello 91, Madrid ⓣ 91 436 3780
United States ⓐ Passeig Reina Elisenda Montcada 23, Barcelona
ⓣ 932 802 227

DRIVING
Breakdown services and motoring information can be obtained from the **Real Automobile Club de Catalunya (RACC)** ⓐ Avenida Diagonal 687 ⓣ 934 955 050 for 24-hour information and emergency breakdown service ⓦ www.racc.es

WHAT'S IN YOUR GUIDEBOOK?

Independent authors Impartial up-to-date information from our travel experts who meticulously source local knowledge.

Experience Thomas Cook's 165 years in the travel industry and guidebook publishing enriches every word with expertise you can trust.

Travel know-how Contributions by thousands of staff around the globe, each one living and breathing travel.

Editors Travel-publishing professionals, pulling everything together to craft a perfect blend of words, pictures, maps and design.

You, the traveller We deliver a practical, no-nonsense approach to information, geared to how you really use it.

SPOT A CITY IN SECONDS

This great range of pocket city guides will have you in the know in no time. Lightweight and packed with detail on the most important things from shopping and sights to non-stop nightlife, they knock spots off chunkier, clunkier versions. Titles include:

HAMBURG

VILNIUS

BILBAO

NEW YORK

GLASGOW

Editorial/project management: Lisa Plumridge
Copy editor: Ismay Atkins
Layout/DTP: Pat Hinsley
Proofreader: Yvonne Bergman

The publishers would like to thank the following individuals and organisations for supplying the copyright photographs for this book: Kirsten Foster, pages 38, 87, 141; Pictures Colour Library, page 124; Victor Puig, pages 16, 22, 40, 63, 67; Eva Serrabassa ©Stockphoto.com, page 46; Pedro Valdeolmillos, page 116; Teresa Fisher, all other photographs.

Send your thoughts to
books@thomascook.com

- Found a great bar, club, shop or must-see sight that we don't feature?
- Like to tip us off about any information that needs a little updating?
- Want to tell us what you love about this handy little guidebook and more importantly how we can make it even handier?

Then here's your chance to tell all! Send us ideas, discoveries and recommendations today and then look out for your valuable input in the next edition of this title.

Email the above address (stating the title) or write to: CitySpots Project Editor, Thomas Cook Publishing, PO Box 227, Coningsby Road, Peterborough PE3 8SB, UK.